Computer Programming Logic Using Flowcharts

Computer Programming Logic Using Flowcharts

Joyce M. Farrell
McHenry County College

A DIVISION OF COURSE TECHNOLOGY
ONE MAIN STREET, CAMBRIDGE, MA 02142

an International Thomson Publishing company I(T)P®

Cambridge • Albany • Bonn • Boston • Cincinnati • London • Madrid • Melbourne • Mexico City
New York • Paris • San Francisco • Singapore • Tokyo • Toronto • Washington

Dedication
For Geoffrey, Andrea, and Audrey

Acquisitions Editor: Anne E. Hamilton
Production Editor: Jean Bermingham
Composition: Gex, Inc.
Interior Design: Gex, Inc.
Cover Design: Diana Coe
Manufacturing Coordinator: Tracy Megison

© 1995 by CTI.
A Division of Course Technology – I(T)P®

For more information contact:

Course Technology
One Main Street
Cambridge, MA 02142

International Thomson Editores
Campos Eliseos 385, Piso 7
Col. Polanco
11560 Mexico D.F. Mexico

International Thomson Publishing Europe
Berkshire House 168-173
High Holborn
London WCIV 7AA
England

International Thomson Publishing GmbH
Königswinterer Strasse 418
53227 Bonn
Germany

Thomas Nelson Australia
102 Dodds Street
South Melbourne, 3205
Victoria, Australia

International Thomson Publishing Asia
211 Henderson Road
#05-10 Henderson Building
Singapore 0315

Nelson Canada
1120 Birchmount Road
Scarborough, Ontario
Canada M1K 5G4

International Thomson Publishing Japan
Hirakawacho Kyowa Building, 3F
2-2-1 Hirakawacho
Chiyoda-ku, Tokyo 102
Japan

ISBN 0-87709-623-6

Printed in the United States of America

10 9 8 7 6 5

Brief Contents

Contents

Preface

Overview

The purpose of this text is to provide students with an introduction to structured programming logic. Flowcharts are used extensively, for I have found them to be an excellent educational tool. The pictorial representation of logical structures makes it significantly easier for the beginning student to identify structured logic as opposed to pseudocode, action diagrams, Nassi-Schneiderman charts, or coding in any programming language.

This text does not attempt to cover systems analysis and design; tools other than flowcharting are more effective for such tasks. Although flowcharts are not the best or most convenient tool for planning programming logic, they are very effective in illustrating the concept of structure for the beginning programmer.

This text may be used to teach programming logic concepts as a prerequisite to a language-specific programming class such as Pascal, BASIC, or C. It can also be used as a companion text to support any language-specific programming text. In general, language-specific programming texts emphasize correct syntax, often at the expense of logic development. *Computer Programming Logic* is the non-language-specific text developed specifically to bridge this gap. The logical flow of statements works in conjunction with any programming language.

Organization

This text was developed from class notes used extensively in teaching a semester Computer Programming Logic class at McHenry County College. The intended audience has no programming background and limited computer experience. The topics are carefully evolved to meet the needs of this student demography. Chapter 1 discusses hardware, software, and other general computer concepts, and provides a review of the concepts taught in a general Introduction to Computers course. Any Introduction to Computers text will cover these topics in more detail.

Flowcharting basics are covered in Chapter 2. The notion of variables is explained, and the student is exposed to the fine line that flowcharts and pseudocode walk between the precision of programming language coding and the ambiguity of English prose.

The concept of structure is introduced in Chapter 3 and reinforced throughout the rest of the book. The student is taught to recognize structure and understand the reasons for it. Chapter 4 expands upon the idea of structure by introducing subroutines and hierarchy charts. Internal and external documentation are covered in Chapter 5, leading to the development of a complete structured program in Chapter 6.

The topics following Chapter 6 may be undertaken in any order. These chapters demonstrate techniques used to solve many common programming problems. The ability to make efficient, correct decisions, to understand when looping is appropriate, and to know how to effect control breaks are valuable tools in many business situations. Arrays increase the efficiency of many computer programs, so the use of arrays is covered thoroughly in Chapter 10. I have always found the discussion of arrays to be one of the times when students get excited with the possibilities of programming. The topic of arrays is expanded upon in Chapter 11's coverage of sorting techniques.

Interactive programming is an important topic for the future microcomputer programmer; techniques for interactive programming and menu handling are presented in Chapter 12. Chapter 13 will be of more interest to the prospective mainframe programmer who will be manipulating sequential files.

Features

This text uses common business examples and avoids mathematical examples and jargon. I have yet to meet anyone in business who needs to write a program to convert Fahrenheit degrees to Celsius or produce a Fibonacci sequence, but business programmers *do* need to produce readable reports with totals at the bottom and numbered pages. Students relate to and understand these business examples more readily than complex mathematical equations that scare them away from programming.

This text avoids technical jargon. I see no reason to mystify the programming process. Words like algorithm and cohesion are discussed, but explained in simple terms. I define "iteration" but in discussion most often refer to "loop."

This text teaches by example. Without numerous examples, the rules as to what makes a problem solution "complete" or a subroutine "good" often go right over students' heads.

The examples and exercises in this text are not overly detailed. The principle of printing a report line can be understood just as well if the line has 3 or 4 fields as if the line has 15 fields. If flowcharting examples go on for many pages, students tend to lose their train of thought.

This text includes thorough skill building exercises at the end of every chapter. Students can listen and read, but they retain most of their understanding by doing real-life applications at the computer (and also have a better time!).

Supplements

An Instructor's Manual is available for adopters of this text. It includes student questions that might come up in the classroom; a suggested time table for covering the material; possible solutions to end-of-chapter exercises; transparency masters for many of the diagrams in the book; and sample test questions.

Acknowledgments

I would like to thank my husband, Geoffrey Farrell, for his help editing this book; Susan Krautstrunk, for creating the original diagrams I needed to beta test the text with my students; Anne Hamilton, Lynn Ulsh, and Jean Bermingham, at boyd & fraser, for their editorial input and assistance; Gex, Inc., for creating the flowchart diagrams; and Dan Dainton, Barbara Ehrhard, Kim Gable, Kathy Lewis, Randy Nease, and Scott Persky, at McHenry County College, who took the time to review the text and/or use it in their classes.

I would also like to thank the following individuals who took time to review the manuscript and propose helpful additions: Bob Forward, Texarkana College; Thomas E. Gorecki, Charles County Community College; Jeffrey Palko, Northwestern State University; William G. Perry, Jr., Western Carolina University; Claude Simpson, Northwestern State University; Paul Svoboda, College of DuPage; and James Thorne, Embry Riddle University.

Joyce Farrell

An Overview of Computer Terminology

Objectives

After studying Chapter 1, you should be able to:

- ► Define basic data processing terms such as hardware and software.
- ► Describe the data processing cycle of input, processing, and output.
- ► Explain the difference between syntax and logical errors.
- ► List the steps involved in producing a computer program.
- ► Describe the data hierarchy of file, record, field, and character.

Computer professionals and hobbyists alike use a common language or jargon when speaking of computer systems. So that everyone reading this book will be on the same wavelength, a brief summary of the most common terms is included here.

Common Terms

Hardware and software are two of the major components of any computer system. **Hardware** is the equipment, or the devices, associated with a computer. In order for a computer to be useful, however, more than equipment is needed. A computer needs instructions. The instructions that tell the computer what to do are called **software**, or programs, and are written by programmers. This book focuses on the process of writing these instructions.

Computer-oriented data processing systems can also be broken down into four major operations:

1. Input
2. Processing
3. Output
4. Storage

Computer hardware by itself doesn't do much until some human provides input in the form of instructions or software, just as your stereo equipment doesn't do much until you provide music on a CD or tape. The instructions to a computer system can be entered through any number of hardware devices such as keyboards, disk drives, or magnetic tape units.

Instructions to a computer are written in a computer **programming language**. Just as some humans speak English and others speak Japanese, programmers write programs in different languages. You may have heard of BASIC, Pascal, COBOL, RPG, C, or Fortran. Some programmers work exclusively in one language; others know several and use the one that seems the most appropriate to the task at the time.

No matter which language a computer programmer uses, the language has rules, which are called its **syntax**. In English, if you ask, "How to store does I get?", most people would probably be able to figure out what you meant, but you have not used proper English syntax. Since computers are not nearly as smart as most humans, you might have well have asked, "Xpwqj mxvxe rthnf djdnm cdf?" Unless the syntax is perfect, the computer cannot interpret the programming language.

All programming languages have translators, sometimes called **compilers** or **interpreters**, that will tell you if you have used a language incorrectly. Therefore, syntax errors are not a big problem. If you write a computer program in a language such as Pascal, but spell one of its words incorrectly or reverse the proper order of two words, the translator lets you know there is a mistake as soon as you try to run the program.

For a program to work properly, the instructions must be given to the computer in a certain order. This is called the **logic** of the computer program. If, in answer to your question of how to get to the store, I tell you, "Go left. Go right. Go three blocks. Go one mile. Get in the car." and those directions are in the wrong sequence, you are going to be pretty confused if not completely lost.

Just as the same directions to the store could be given in French or German or Spanish, the same logic of a program can be expressed in any number of programming languages. This book is almost exclusively concerned with this logic process. We are not concerned with any specific language, so this book could have been written in Japanese or BASIC or COBOL. The logic would be the same in any language. For convenience, English will be used!

Once instructions have been input to the computer, a program can be **run** or **executed**. A computer program that would take a number, double it, and tell you the answer could be written in Pascal or C, but if it were written in English, it would look like this:

Get number
*Answer = number * 2*
Print answer

(Programmers often use * to mean multiplication and / to mean division.)

This program illustrates the first three of the four major computer operations—input, processing, and output. The instruction to Get number is an example of an input operation. When the computer interprets this instruction, it knows to look to an input device to obtain a number. Computers often have several input devices such as a keyboard and two disk drives. When you learn a specific programming language, you learn how to tell the computer which of those input devices to look to. For now, however, it doesn't really matter which hardware device is used as long as a number is obtained.

Processing then occurs when the mathematics is done to double the number: Answer = number * 2. Mathematical operations are not the only kind of processing, but they are a very typical kind of processing.

In the preceding program, output is represented by the Print answer statement. Again, within a particular program, this might mean to the monitor or to the printer, but the process is the same.

Besides input, processing, and output, the fourth operation in any computer system is storage. Storage comes in two broad categories. All computers have **internal storage** probably referred to more often as **memory**, **main memory**, or **primary memory**. This storage is inside the machine and is the type of storage most often discussed in this book. Computers also have **external storage**, which is storage outside the main memory of the machine on some device such as a floppy disk, hard disk, or magnetic tape. Both programs and data are stored on these media.

To run, computer programs must be loaded into memory first. A program might be typed into memory from the keyboard, or it might be already written and stored on a disk. Either way, a copy of the instructions must be placed in memory before the program can be run.

Both internal memory and external storage are necessary. Internal memory is needed in order to run the programs, but internal memory is **volatile**, that is, its contents are lost every time the computer is shut off. Therefore, if a program is going to be used more than once, it must be stored, or **saved**, on some nonvolatile medium so that it is not lost forever when the computer is turned off. External storage—disks or tape—provides that nonvolatile medium.

Once a copy of the program is in memory, any data that the program needs must also be placed into main memory. For example, after the program

Get number
*Answer = number * 2*
Print answer

is placed into memory and starts to run, an actual number, say, 8, also needs to be placed into memory. It is placed into memory in a location that the program will call number. Then, and only then, can the answer, in this case, 16, be calculated and printed.

The Programming Process

It is the job of the programmer to write instructions such as the three instructions in the doubling program in the preceding section. A programmer's job can be broken down into six distinct steps:

1. Understand the problem.
2. Plan the logic.
3. Code the program.
4. Translate the program into machine language.
5. Test the program.
6. Put the program into production.

Understand the Problem

Programmers on the job are writing programs to satisfy the needs of others—the personnel department that needs a printed list of all employees, the billing department that wants a list of clients who are 30 or more days overdue in their payments, or the office manager who would like to be notified when specific supplies reach the reorder point. Since programmers are providing a service to these users, programmers must first understand what it is the users want.

Suppose the personnel office says to a programmer, "We need a list of all employees who have been here over five years because we want to invite them to a special thank-you dinner." On the surface this seems like a simple enough request. An experienced programmer, however, will know that he or she may not yet understand the whole problem. Do they want a list of full-time employees only or one of full- and part-time employees? Do they want people who have worked for us on a contractual basis over the last five years or regular employees only? Do they need to be working for us for five years as of today or as of the date of the dinner, or is some other date to be used as a cut off? What about an employee who worked here three years, took a two-year leave of absence, and has been back for three years. Does he or she qualify? None of these decisions can be made by the programmer—the user is the one to whom these questions must be addressed.

What does the user want the report of five-year employees to look like? Should it contain both first and last names? Social security numbers? Phone numbers? Addresses? Is all this data available? Several pieces of documentation are often provided to the programmer to help him or her understand the problem. These include print layout charts and file specifications, which will be discussed in Chapter 4.

Really understanding the problem may be one of the most difficult aspects of programming. On any job, the description of what is needed may be vague, or worse yet, the user may not even really know what it is he or she wants. A good programmer is part counselor, part detective!

Plan the Logic

During this phase of the programming process, the programmer plans the steps to the program. There are many ways to plan the solution to a problem (you may hear programmers refer to it as "developing an algorithm"), but the two most common tools are flowcharts and pseudocode. Both tools involve writing down the steps of the program in English, much as you would plan a trip on paper before buying clothes for it, or plan your purchases for a party before going shopping for food.

The programmer doesn't worry about the syntax of any language at this point, just the sequence of events that will lead from available input to desired output. Much more will be said about this planning of the logic later; in fact, this book focuses on this step almost exclusively.

Code the Program

Once the logic of a program has been developed, then, and only then, can the program be written in one of the over 400 programming languages that exist. It is at this point that the programmer can worry about each command being spelled correctly and all of the punctuation getting into the right spots; in other words, using the correct *syntax*.

Some very experienced programmers can successfully combine the logic planning and the actual instruction writing, or **coding** of the program, in one step. This may work for very simple programs, just as you can plan and write a postcard to your friend in one step. A term paper, however, needs planning before writing, and so do most programs.

Which is the harder step, planning or coding? Right now, it may seem to you that writing in a programming language is a very difficult task, considering all the spelling and grammar rules to learn. However, the planning step is actually more difficult. Which is more difficult, thinking up the twists and turns to the plot of a best-selling mystery novel or writing a translation of an already-written novel from English to Spanish? And who do you think gets paid more, the writer or the translator?

Translate the Program into Machine Language

Even though there are many programming languages, all computers know only one language, and that language, sometimes called **machine language**, consists of many little 1's and 0's. Computers understand this machine language because computers themselves are made up of thousands of tiny electrical switches that can be set in either the on or off state, which is often represented by a 1 or 0, respectively.

Languages like Pascal or BASIC are available for us only because someone has written a translator program (often called a compiler or interpreter) that changes the **high-level language** in which we write into machine language. The translator program catches all syntax errors.

If there were an English compiler to which I could submit the sentence `The grl go to school`, it would point out two syntax errors to me. The second word, `grl`, would be illegal because it is not part of the English language. Once I corrected the word to `girl`, the compiler would find another syntax error on the third word, `go`, because it was the wrong verb for the subject `girl`. This doesn't mean `go` is necessarily the wrong word. Maybe `girl` is wrong; perhaps I meant to say `girls` in which case `go` is right. Compilers don't always know exactly what you meant, but they do know when something is wrong with your syntax.

Test the Program

A program that is free of syntax errors is not necessarily free of **logical errors**. The sentence The girl goes to school, although syntactically perfect, is not logically correct if the girl is a baby or a drop-out.

Once a program is free of syntax errors, it can be tested; that is, executed with some sample data to see whether or not the results are logically correct. Recall this program:

> *Get number*
> *Answer = number * 2*
> *Print answer*

If the number 2 is given to the program and the number 4 prints out, I have run one successful test on the program.

If, however, the number 40 prints out, maybe it's because I have a logical error in my program. Even though I intended to write

> *Get number*
> *Answer = number * 2*
> *Print answer*

maybe I actually coded

> *Get number*
> *Answer = number * 20*
> *Print answer*

and the error of placing 20 in the multiplication statement instead of 2 has caused the logical error. Notice that nothing is syntactically wrong with this second program—it is just as reasonable to multiply a number by 20 as by 2—but if I intended to only double the number, a logical error has occurred.

It is always important to test the program with as many examples as seem reasonable. For example, if I write the program to double a number and enter 2 and get a 4, it doesn't mean I have a correct program. Perhaps I have typed this program by mistake:

> *Get number*
> *Answer = number + 2*
> *Print answer*

An input of 2 results in an answer of 4, but it doesn't mean my program doubles numbers—it actually only adds 2 to them. If I test my program with additional data, say, a 3, as soon as I see the answer 5, I know I have a problem.

Selecting test data is somewhat of an art in itself, and it should be done carefully. If personnel wants a list of names of five-year employees, it would be a mistake to test my program with a small sample file of only long-term employees. If no new employees are tested, I don't really know if my program would have eliminated them from the list.

Put the Program into Production

Once the program has been tested adequately, the organization can use it. This might involve running the program once if the program was written to satisfy a user's request for a special list, or this might be a process that takes months if the program will be run regularly from now on. Perhaps data entry people must be trained to prepare the input, users must be trained to understand the output, and existing data in the company must be changed to some entirely new format to accommodate this program. **Conversion** to a new program or set of programs can sometimes take an organization months or years to accomplish.

Data Hierarchy

One last set of terminology needs to be discussed. When data is stored for use on computer systems, it is often stored in what is known as a **hierarchy**.

The smallest usable unit of data is the **character**. Characters are letters, numbers, and special symbols such as "A", "7", and "$". Basically, if you can type it from the keyboard in one keystroke, it is a character. Characters are made up of smaller elements called **bits**, but just as most humans can use a pencil without caring whether or not atoms are flying around inside it, most computer users can store characters without caring about these bits.

Characters are often grouped together to make up **fields**. A field is a group of characters with some meaning. For most of us, an "S", an "M", an "I", a "T", and an "H" don't have much meaning individually, but if the group of characters "SMITH" is your last name, then you have useful meaning. These characters might comprise a field called NAME. Other fields with meaning to you might be called ADDRESS or SALARY.

Fields are often grouped together into **records**. Records are groups of fields that go together for some logical reason. A random name, address, and salary aren't very useful, but if they're your name, your address, and your salary, then that's your record—and we can mail you a check.

Records, in turn, are grouped together to make **files**. Files are groups of records that go together for some logical reason. The individual records of each student in your class might go together in a file called CLASS. Records of each person at your company might be in a file called PERSONNEL. Items you sell might be in INVENTORY.

Some files can have just a few records; others, like the file of credit card holders for a major department store chain or policy holders of a major insurance company, can have thousands or even millions of records.

To be able to discuss data needs with computer professionals, it is important to understand this relationship of data, or **data hierarchy**:

File
Record
Field
Character

TERMS AND CONCEPTS

hardware

software

input

processing

output

storage

syntax vs. logical errors

compilers and interpreters

internal and external storage

programming steps

file

record

field

character

EXERCISES

ex. *Exercise 1* **Matching**

Match the definition with the appropriate term.

_____ 1. The equipment of a computer system	**a.** compiler
_____ 2. Another word for programs	**b.** syntax
_____ 3. Language rules	**c.** logic
_____ 4. Order of instructions	**d.** hardware
_____ 5. Language translator	**e.** software

ex. *Exercise 2*

a. Suggest a good set of test data to use for a program that gives an employee a $50 bonus check if more than 1000 units have been produced in a week.

b. Suggest a good set of test data for a program that computes gross paychecks based on hours worked and rate of pay. The program computes gross as hours times rate unless hours are over 40. Then the program computes gross as hours times 40, plus hours over 40 times one and a half times rate.

c. Suggest a good set of test data for a program that is intended to output a student's grade point average based on grades in five courses.

ex. *Exercise 3*

In your own words, describe the steps to writing a computer program.

ex. *Exercise 4*

a. Assume a file is kept for a grocery store inventory, one record for each grocery item. Name at least 10 fields that might be stored for each record.

b. Assume a file is kept for a library collection, one record for each item the library loans out. Name at least 10 fields that might be stored for each record.

Introduction to Flowcharting

Objectives

After studying Chapter 2, you should be able to:

▶ Identify and appropriately use the basic flowcharting symbols.

▶ Explain the differences between flowcharts and pseudocode.

▶ Define a variable.

▶ Explain how to define or declare a variable.

▶ Explain the difference between character and numeric variables.

▶ Use a dummy, or sentinel, value.

▶ Recognize the proper format of assignment statements.

When programmers plan the logic for a solution to a programming problem, they often use one of two tools, flowcharts or pseudocode. A **flowchart** is a pictorial representation of the logical steps it takes to solve a problem. **Pseudocode** is an English-like representation of the same thing. If you know that "pseudo" is a prefix that means false and you know that to "code" a program is to put it in a programming language, then pseudocode simply means "false code," or sentences that appear to have been written in a computer programming language but don't necessarily follow all the syntax rules of that language.

Professional programmers use flowcharts less often than pseudocode because once a programmer thoroughly understands the logic of processing data, it often becomes too time consuming to draw pictures to represent the logical flow. Many programmers do flowchart, however, and flowcharts are an excellent tool for the beginner to visualize how the statements in a program are interrelated.

Flowcharting Basics

Almost every program involves the steps of input, processing, and output, as in the program

> *Get number*
> *Answer = number * 2*
> *Print answer*

Therefore, most flowcharts need some way to visually separate these three steps. Drawing different boxes around the statements is the standard convention.

Input operations are represented by the parallelogram. A statement is written in English, inside the parallelogram, as shown in Figure 2.1.

FIGURE 2.1

Get
Number

Arithmetic statements are examples of processing statements. Processing statements are represented in flowcharts by rectangles, and statements are written inside of them, as shown in Figure 2.2.

FIGURE 2.2

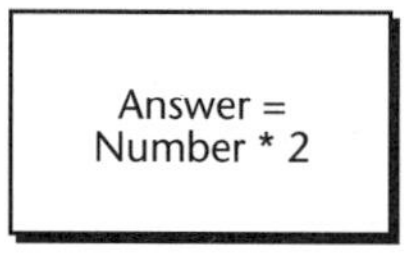

Answer =
Number * 2

Output statements use the same symbol as input statements—the parallelogram, as in Figure 2.3.

FIGURE 2.3

Print
Answer

To show the correct sequence of these statements, arrows (or flowlines) are used to connect the steps. Whenever possible, most of a flowchart should read from top to bottom or from left to right on a page. That's the natural way we read English, so that's not a very hard rule to follow!

To be complete, a flowchart should include two more elements: a terminal or start/stop symbol at each end. Usually a word like **START** or **BEGIN** is placed in the first terminal symbol and a word like **END** or **STOP** is placed in the other. The standard terminal symbol is shaped like a race track ( ). Figure 2.4 shows a complete flowchart for the program that doubles a number.

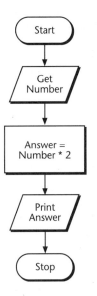

► FIGURE 2.4

The logic for this program is correct no matter what programming language is used. The programmer now only needs to buy a computer, learn a language, code the program, compile it, test it, and put it into production.

"Whoa!" you are probably saying to yourself. "This is simply not worth it! All that work to create a flowchart and *then* all those other steps!? For five bucks I can buy a pocket calculator that will double any number for me!" You are absolutely right. If this were a real computer program, it simply would not be worth all the effort. Writing a computer program would only be worth the effort if you had many, let's say one thousand, numbers to find the double of in a limited amount of time, let's say the next fifteen minutes. Then it would be worth your while to have a computer program.

Our program

Get number
*Answer = number * 2*
Print answer

unfortunately does not double one thousand numbers. It only doubles one. The program could be run one thousand times, of course, but that would require a human to sit at the computer telling it to run the program over and over again. We would be better off with a program that could process one thousand numbers, one after the other.

One solution would be to write the program as

Get number
*Answer = number * 2*
Print answer
Get number
*Answer = number * 2*
Print answer
Get number
*Answer = number * 2*
Print answer....

This would be very time consuming, and again, you might as well buy the calculator.

A better solution would be to have the computer execute the same set of three instructions over and over again. That could be represented pictorially as shown in Figure 2.5. With this approach, the computer gets a number, doubles it, prints out the answer, and then starts over again with the first instruction. The same spot in memory, called NUMBER, is reused for the second number and for any subsequent numbers. ANSWER is reused each time to store the result of the multiplication operation.

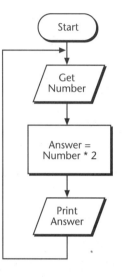

FIGURE 2.5

Variables

Programmers commonly refer to the locations in memory called NUMBER and ANSWER as **variables**. Variables are memory locations, the contents of which can vary. Sometimes NUMBER can hold a 2 and ANSWER a 4; other times NUMBER can hold a 6 and ANSWER a 12. It is the ability of memory variables to change in value that makes computers and programming worthwhile. Because one memory location can be used over and over again with different values, program instructions can be written once and then used for thousands of problems. *One* set of payroll instructions at your company produces each individual's paycheck, and *one* set of instructions at your electric company produces each household's bill.

Our flowchart example has two variables, NUMBER and ANSWER. These could just as well have been named ENTRY and SOLUTION, or VALUE and TWICEVALUE. Every computer programming language has its own set of rules for naming variables. The different languages put different limits on the length of variable names. Some languages allow hyphens in variable names; others allow underscores; still others allow neither. Some languages allow dollar signs in variable names; others do not.

For example, in some very old versions of BASIC, a variable name could consist of only one or two letters and one or two numbers. You could have some cryptic variable names like N3 or AN or RE02. In other languages, variable names can be very long. COBOL, for example, allows up to 30 characters in its variable names, so names like AMOUNT-OF-SALE and TOTAL-FOR-JANUARY are not uncommon. COBOL allows hyphens in its variable names for better readability. Another language, C, usually uses lowercase letters, doesn't allow hyphens, but does allow underscores, so a name like price_of_item could be used.

Even though every language has its own rules for naming variables, when designing the logic of a computer program, you should not concern yourself with the particular syntax of any language. The logic, after all, works with any language. Variable names throughout this book follow only two rules:

1. *Variable names must be one word*. That one word can contain letters, numbers, hyphens, underscores, or any other characters I choose, with one exception—there are to be *no spaces*. Therefore, R is a legal variable name as is RATE as is INTEREST-RATE. The variable name INTEREST RATE is not allowed because of the space. If I saw INTEREST RATE in a flowchart, I would assume that the programmer was discussing two variables, INTEREST and RATE, each of which individually would be a fine variable name.

2. *Variable names must have some meaning*. This is not a rule of any programming language. If you really were computing an interest rate in a program, the computer wouldn't care if you called the variable G or U84 or FRED. As long as the correct numeric result was placed in the variable, its actual name doesn't really matter. However it's going to be much easier to follow the logic of a program that has a statement in it like

   *TOTAL = INVESTMENT * INTEREST-RATE*

than one that has a statement in it like

   *BANANA = J89 * LINDA*

Notice that the flowchart in Figure 2.5 follows these two rules for variables: both variable names, NUMBER and ANSWER, are one word, and they have some meaning.

EOF

Something is still wrong with the flowchart for doubling numbers. It never ends! The computer will keep accepting numbers and printing out doubles forever. Of course, I could refuse to give it any more numbers. The computer is very patient, and if I refuse to give it any more numbers, it will sit and wait forever. However, since I can't do anything else with the computer while it is sitting and waiting, this is not a good solution. Another solution would be to simply turn the computer off! That'll fix it! But, again, it's not the best way.

The best way to end the program is to have some predetermined value for NUMBER that means "Stop the program!" For example, the programmer and the user could agree that the user will never need to know the double of 0, so the user could enter a 0 when he or she wanted to stop. The computer could then test any incoming value for NUMBER and, if it is a 0, stop the program.

Decisions are represented in flowcharts by diamonds. The diamond usually contains a question, the answer to which is either yes or no. All good computer questions have two mutually exclusive answers like yes and no. For example, "When is your birthday?" is not a good computer question because there are 366 possible answers. But, "Is your birthday June 24?" *is* a good computer question because for everyone in the world, the answer is yes or no.

The question to stop our doubling program will be "Is the number just entered equal to 0?" The complete flowchart will now look like the one shown in Figure 2.6.

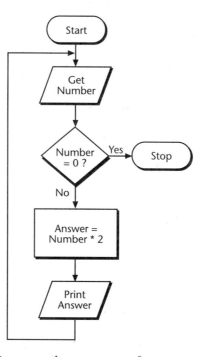

FIGURE 2.6

One drawback to using 0 to stop the program, of course, is that it won't work if the user *does* need to find the double of 0. Then some other value that the user never will need, such as 999 or –1 could be selected to signal that the program should end. A preselected value is often called a **dummy value** because it is there not as real data, but just as a signal to stop. Sometimes it is called a **sentinel value** because it represents an entry or exit point.

When incoming data is stored on a disk or tape, the computer can recognize the end of the data automatically, without a dummy value, through a code that is stored at the end of the data. Many programmers would use the term **EOF** (for "end of file") to talk about this marker. This book therefore uses EOF to indicate the end of data, regardless of whether it is a special disk marker or a dummy value like 0. Therefore, the flowchart now looks like the one in Figure 2.7.

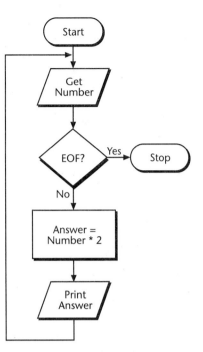

FIGURE 2.7

The Connector

Using just the input, processing, output, decision, and terminal symbols allows us to represent the logic of abundant and diverse applications. This book uses only one other symbol, a connector. A connector will be used when the physical constraints of page size stop me from completing a flowchart. If a flowchart had six processing steps and I had only room for three on a page, I might represent the logic as shown in Figure 2.8.

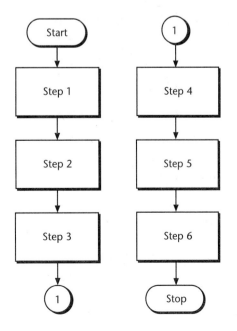

FIGURE 2.8

The circle at the bottom of the left column tells someone reading the flowchart that there is more. The circle should contain a number or letter that can then be matched to another number or letter somewhere else, in this case, on the right. If a large flow-chart needs more connectors new numbers or letters would be assigned in sequence (1,2,3... or A,B,C...) to each successive pair.

Format of Mathematical Statements

According to the rules of algebra, a statement like

*ANSWER = NUMBER * 2*

should be exactly equivalent to the statement

*NUMBER * 2 = ANSWER*

To most programmers, however, `ANSWER = NUMBER * 2` means something different. It means multiply NUMBER by 2 and store the result in the variable called ANSWER. Whatever operation is performed to the right of the equal sign results in a value that is placed in the memory location to the left of the equal sign. Therefore the statement

*NUMBER * 2 = ANSWER*

would attempt to take the value of ANSWER and store it in a location called NUMBER * 2. There is no such location. There is a location called NUMBER, but there can't be a location called NUMBER * 2. For one thing, NUMBER * 2 can't be a variable because it has spaces in it. For another, a location can't be multiplied. Its contents can be multiplied, but the location itself cannot be.

Computer memory is made up of thousands of distinct locations, each of which has an address. Forty years ago, programmers had to deal with these addresses and had to remember, for instance, that they had stored a salary in location 6428 of their computer. Nowadays we are very fortunate that high-level computer languages have been developed that allow us to pick a reasonable "English" name for a memory address and let the computer keep track of where it is. Just as it is easier for you to remember that the president lives in the WHITE HOUSE than at 1600 Pennsylvania Avenue, Washington, D.C., it is also easier for you to remember that your salary is in a variable called SALARY than at memory location 6428.

Just like street addresses, it does not usually make sense to do mathematical operations on memory addresses, but it does make sense to do mathematical operations on the *contents* of memory addresses. If you live in BLUE-SPLIT-LEVEL-ON-THE-CORNER, you can't add 1 to that, but you certainly can add 1 person to the contents of that house. For our purposes, then, the statement

*ANSWER = NUMBER * 2*

means exactly the same thing as the statement

*MOVE NUMBER * 2 to ANSWER*

which also means exactly the same thing as the statement

MULTIPLY NUMBER TIMES 2 GIVING ANSWER

None of these statements, however, is equivalent to

*NUMBER * 2 = ANSWER*

which we will consider an illegal statement.

Types of Variables

Most computer languages have at least two distinct types of variables. One type of variable can hold a number and is often called a **numeric variable**. In the statement

*ANSWER = NUMBER * 2*

both ANSWER and NUMBER are numeric variables, that is, their intended contents are numeric values such as 6 and 3, 150 and 75, or –18 and –9.

Most languages have a separate type of variable that can hold letters of the alphabet and other special characters such as punctuation marks. Depending on the language, these variables are called **character**, **text**, or **string variables**. If a program had the statement

NAME = "WASHINGTON"

it would be assumed that NAME was a character variable.

We must distinguish between numeric and character variables because computers handle the two types of data differently. Therefore, means are provided within the syntax rules of computer programming languages to tell the computer which type of data is expected. How this is done is different in every language; in some languages there are different rules for naming the variables, but in others a simple statement (called a **declaration**) telling the computer which type to expect is enough.

Some languages allow for additional types of data. Languages like Pascal and C distinguish between integer or whole number numeric variables and floating-point, decimal, or fractional numeric variables. Thus, in some languages, the numbers 4 and 4.3 would have to be stored in different type variables.

Other languages include special types for logical or Boolean variables, which can have only one of two values—true or false.

The character versus numeric distinction is universal, however, and is the only variable distinction that this book makes. If a variable called RATE is supposed to hold a value of 2.5, we will assume that it is a numeric variable. If a variable called ITEM is supposed to hold a value of "TYPEWRITER," we will assume that it is character. By convention, character data like "TYPEWRITER" is included in quotes to distinguish it from yet another variable name. According to our conventions then

PRICE = 159.75   and   *ITEM = "TYPEWRITER"*

would both be valid statements.

ITEM = TYPEWRITER

would be a valid statement only if a variable named TYPEWRITER had been assigned a value previously, as in

TYPEWRITER = "REMINGTON"

The two statements

TYPEWRITER = "REMINGTON"   and   *ITEM = TYPEWRITER*

then would have the same final result as

ITEM = "REMINGTON"

TERMS AND CONCEPTS

flowchart

pseudocode

symbols:

input-output (parallelogram), process (rectangle), terminal (racetrack), decision (diamond), connector (circle)

variable

dummy (sentinel) value

EOF

format of mathematical or assignment statements

numeric and character variables

declaration

EXERCISES

ex. *Exercise 1* **Matching**

Match the term with the appropriate shape.

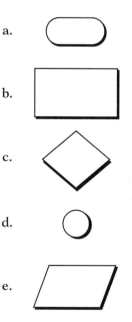

_____ **1.** decision   **a.**

_____ **2.** input/output   **b.**

_____ **3.** terminal   **c.**

_____ **4.** process   **d.**

_____ **5.** connector   **e.**

ex. *Exercise 2*

Which of the following names seem like good variable names to you? If a name doesn't seem like a good variable name, why not?

  a. C
  b. COST
  c. COST-AMOUNT
  d. COST AMOUNT
  e. CSTOFDOINGBSNS
  f. COST-OF-DOING-BUSINESS-THIS-FISCAL-YEAR

ex. *Exercise 3*

If AGE, and RATE are numeric variables and DEPT is a character variable, which of the following statements are valid assignments? If not valid, why not?

  a. AGE = 23
  b. AGE = RATE
  c. AGE = DEPT
  d. AGE = "DEPT"
  e. 42 = AGE
  f. RATE = 3.5
  g. RATE = AGE
  h. RATE = DEPT
  i. 6.91 = RATE
  j. DEPT = PERSONNEL
  k. DEPT = "PERSONNEL"
  l. DEPT = 413
  m. DEPT = "413"
  n. DEPT = AGE
  o. DEPT = RATE
  p. 413 = DEPT
  q. "413" = DEPT

Structure

Objectives

After studying Chapter 3, you should be able to:

- ▶ Explain the difference between structured and unstructured logic.
- ▶ Describe the three basic structures of sequence, selection, and loop.
- ▶ Describe two other optional structures.
- ▶ Understand the necessity for the priming read.

Real programs usually get far more complicated than

> *Get number*
> *Answer = number * 2*
> *Print answer*

Imagine the program that NASA uses to calculate the angle of launch of a space shuttle, or the program the IRS uses to audit your income tax return. Even the program that produces a paycheck for you on your job is made up of many, many instructions. Designing the logic to such a program can be a time-consuming task.

Spaghetti Code

Let's take a fairly simple task. You are in charge of admissions at a college, and you've decided you will admit prospective students on the following criteria:

- You will admit students who score 90 or better on the admission test your college gives as long as they are in the upper 75% of their high school graduating class. (These are smart students who maybe didn't do so well in high school but probably have matured.)
- You will admit students who score at least 80 on the admission test if they are in the upper 50% of their high school graduating class.
- You will admit students who score only 70 on your test if they are in the top 25% of their class. (These are students who maybe don't take tests well but obviously are achievers.)

Here, then, is a summary of the admission requirements:

Test Score	High School Rank (%)
90+	25+
80+	50+
70+	75+

The flowchart for this program could look like the one in Figure 3.1. This kind of flowchart has a special name—**spaghetti code**. The reason should be obvious—it's as confusing to follow as following one noodle through a plate of spaghetti.

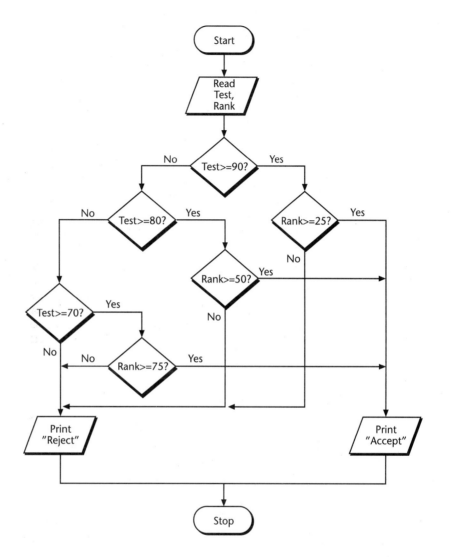

FIGURE 3.1

The Structures

Many computer programs that were written from about 1950 to 1980 bore a striking resemblance to the preceding flowchart. The programs worked, that is, they produced the correct result, but they were very difficult to read and maintain and their logic was difficult to follow.

In the mid-1960s, mathematicians proved that any program, no matter how complicated, could be solved using only three sets of flowcharting shapes—or **structures**. With these three structures alone, any event, from doubling a number to performing brain surgery, could be diagrammed.

The first of these structures is called a **sequence**, as shown in Figure 3.2. You do something, you do something else, you do something else. A sequence can have any number of events, but if one step follows another with no chance to branch off, a series of events is a sequence.

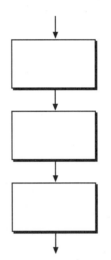

FIGURE 3.2

The second structure is called a **selection**, or a **decision**, as shown in Figure 3.3. In this structure, a question is asked and, depending on the answer, one of two steps is taken. Then, no matter which path is followed, the logic comes back together and continues on.

Some people call this structure an **if-then-else** because it fits the statement

IF condition is true THEN do one process ELSE do the other

For example,

if HOURS-WORKED is more than 40 then CALCULATE-OVERTIME else CALCULATE-REGULAR-TIME.

Note that it is perfectly all right for one branch of the selection to be "do nothing." An example might be,

if BONUS = "yes" then add $50 to GROSS.

That's it—don't do anything if BONUS is not "yes." The case where nothing is done is often called the **null case**.

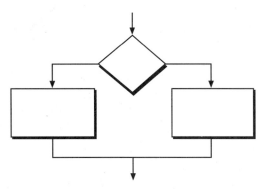

FIGURE 3.3

The third structure is called a **loop**, although you may hear it referred to as **repetition** or **iteration**, as shown in Figure 3.4. In the loop, a question is asked. If the answer is such that a step needs to be performed, the step is performed and then the original question is asked again. Perhaps the step is executed again, and then the original question is asked again. This continues until the answer to the question is such that the step no longer needs to be performed, and then the structure is exited.

Some call this structure a **do while** because it fits the statement

WHILE test condition continues to be true, DO process

For example, while inventory remains low, continue to order more and ask again; or while there are more numbers to be doubled, print an answer and ask again.

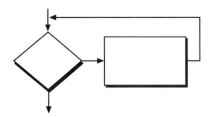

FIGURE 3.4

All logic problems can be solved using only these three structures. These three structures, of course, can be combined in an infinite number of ways. There can be a sequence of steps followed by a selection, or a loop followed by a sequence.

Most important, any individual step in the preceding structure diagrams can itself be replaced with yet another structure—any sequence, selection, or loop.

For example, you could have a sequence of three steps on one side of a selection, as shown in Figure 3.5.

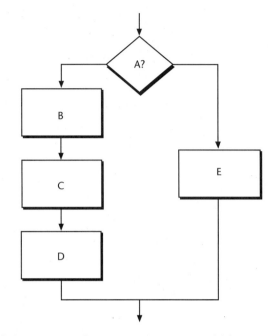

In place of one of the steps in that sequence, you could have a selection. In Figure 3.6, step C has been replaced with a selection structure.

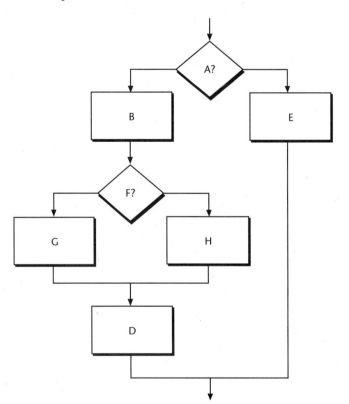

In place of the step on one side of that selection, inside the sequence, inside the selection, you could have a loop. In Figure 3.7, step H from Figure 3.6 has been replaced with a loop structure.

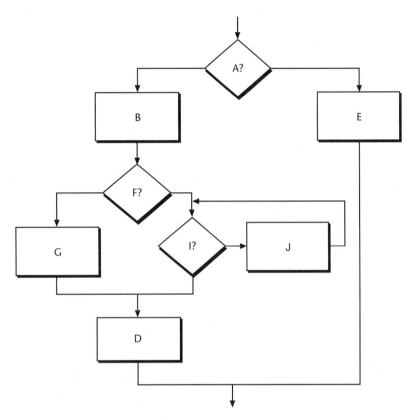

FIGURE 3.7

The combinations are endless, but as long as a flowchart can be broken down into the basic structures, the whole flowchart is structured.

The Priming Read

In Chapter 2, we discussed a program that looked like the one in Figure 3.8.

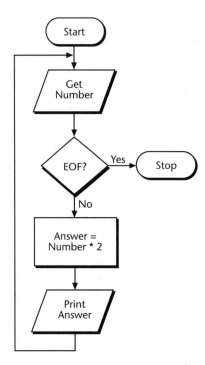

FIGURE 3.8

Is this program structured? At first, it may be hard to tell. The three allowed structures are illustrated in Figure 3.9.

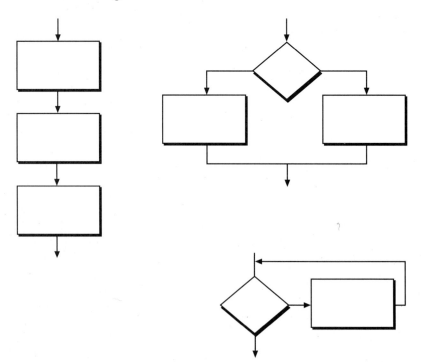

FIGURE 3.9

If the flowchart of the doubling problem can be redrawn so that the "yes" side of the EOF decision goes down and the "no" side goes to the right, it may look more like one or more of the three structures. See Figure 3.10

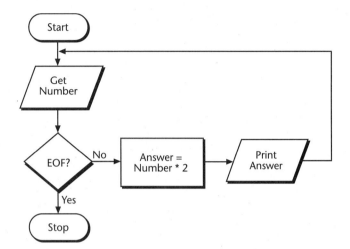

FIGURE 3.10

Still, is it structured? Let's take one step at a time. The beginning of the flowchart looks like Figure 3.11.

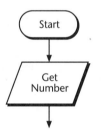

FIGURE 3.11

Is this much of the flowchart structured? Sure, it's a sequence. The next part of the flowchart looks like Figure 3.12.

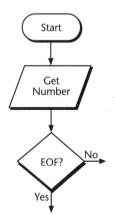

FIGURE 3.12

The sequence is over. Either a selection is starting or a loop is starting. You may not know which one, but you do know it can't be a sequence any more because sequences can't have questions in them. So, which is it, a selection or a loop?

In a selection structure, the logic goes in one of two directions after the question is asked. Then it comes back together again; the question is not asked a second time.

In a loop, if the procedure is executed, the question is always asked again.

In the doubling problem, if it is not EOF, that is, if the end-of-file condition is not met, some math is done, an answer is printed, a new number is obtained, and the EOF question is asked again. So, the doubling problem is more like a loop than a selection.

It *is* a loop, but it's not a structured loop. In a structured loop, the rule is: a question is asked, a procedure is done, and you go right back to the question. Our flowchart does more than one thing. It does math, then it prints, but it doesn't go right back to the question. Instead, it goes above the question to get another number.

The fact that the flowchart does two things, math and printing, is no problem because those two things are a structure in themselves, a sequence structure—and we've already said it's all right to have a structure within a structure. What's wrong is for the logic to go above the question to get another number. The correct structure is for the logic to return to the question.

The flowchart in Figure 3.13 then would be structured, but it has one big problem. It doesn't do the job of continuously doubling numbers.

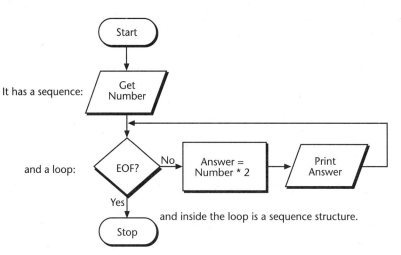

FIGURE 3.13

Suppose when the program is started someone enters a 9. It's not EOF, so the number is doubled, 18 is printed out as the answer, and the question EOF is asked. It can't be EOF because the dummy or ending value could never be entered since the GET NUMBER step was never returned to. Therefore 9 is doubled again and the answer, 18, is printed again. It's still not EOF, so the same steps are repeated again. This goes on *forever*.

Therefore, the program logic shown in Figure 3.14 is structured, but it doesn't work; the program in Figure 3.15 works, but it isn't structured!

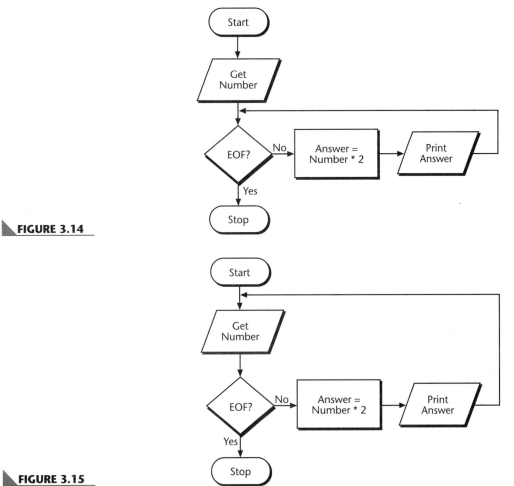

FIGURE 3.14

FIGURE 3.15

What's the solution? Often, for a program to be structured, something extra has to be added. In this case, it's an extra GET NUMBER step. Consider the solution in Figure 3.16. It's structured, *and* it does what it's supposed to!

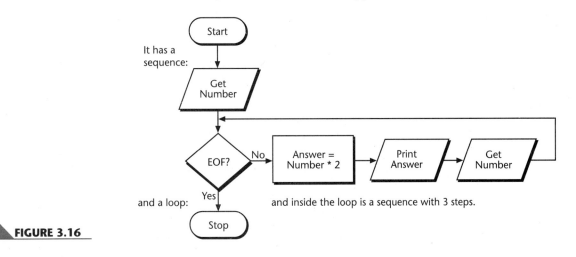

FIGURE 3.16

The extra GET NUMBER step is typical in structured programs. The first of the two input steps is often called a **priming input**, or **priming read**—"priming" as in "primary" (or as in "priming the pump") and "input," or "read," as common computer language verbs used for input.

Reasons for Structure

At this point, you may very well be saying, "I liked the original doubling program just fine. I could follow it. Also, the first program had one less step in it, so it was less work. Who cares if a program is structured?"

Since you haven't had much programming experience, you are just going to have to take my word for it for now that structured is better for the following reasons:

1. Clarity—The doubling program is a small program. As programs get bigger, they get more confusing if they're not structured.

2. Professionalism—All other programmers (and programming teachers you may encounter) expect your programs to be structured. It's the way things are done in the 1990s.

3. Efficiency—Most newer computer languages are structured languages whose syntax lets you deal with these structures efficiently. Even older languages like assembler, COBOL, and RPG, that were developed before the principles of structured programming, can be written in a structured form and are expected to be written that way today.

4. Modularity—Structured programs can be easily broken into routines which can be assigned to any number of programmers. The routines are then pieced back together like modular furniture. Notice in Figure 3.17 that all three structures have one entry and one exit point.

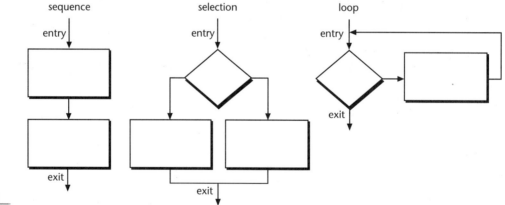

FIGURE 3.17

One programmer's structured code can attach nicely to another's at these end points. If the programmers were using spaghetti code there would be too many crossed wires to worry about; coordinating efforts would become very difficult. Modularity allows distinct subprograms to attach to one another with a minimum of problems.

Most programs today are huge. If you've worked with a program like WordPerfect or Lotus 1-2-3 you can imagine the number of instructions that went into writing those programs. Needless to say, they are not the work of one programmer. The modular nature of structured programs means that work can be divided among many programmers, so that the program is written much more quickly. Money is often a motivating factor. A program that is written more quickly is available for use sooner, and can start making money for the developer sooner.

Consider the college admission program from the beginning of the chapter. It has been rewritten in structured form in Figure 3.18. Doesn't it look easier to follow now?

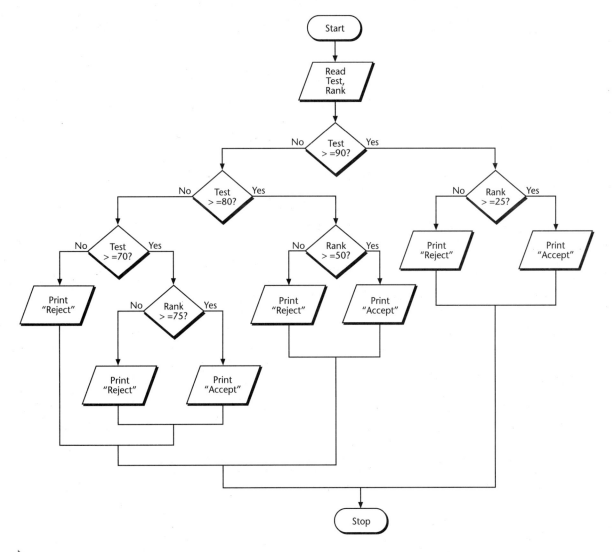

 FIGURE 3.18

Recognizing Structure

Is the flowchart segment in Figure 3.19 structured?

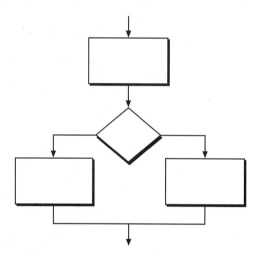

FIGURE 3.19

Yes, it is. It has a sequence and a selection structure.

Is the flowchart segment in Figure 3.20 structured?

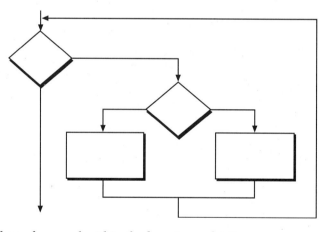

FIGURE 3.20

Yes, it is. It has a loop and within the loop is a selection.

Is the flowchart segment in Figure 3.21 structured?

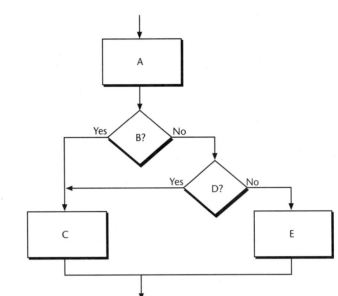

FIGURE 3.21

No, it isn't. One way to straighten out a flowchart that isn't structured is to use what I call the "spaghetti bowl" method: grab one piece of pasta at the top of the bowl, place it in your mouth, and keep slurping it in until it is untangled. For example, in Figure 3.21, if you start pulling at the top, you get a procedure box (step A). See Figure 3.22. That's okay; it's structured. Keep pulling.

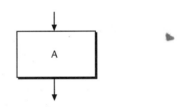

FIGURE 3.22

Next comes a question (B). If you pull up on the left side of the question only, a box pops up (C). See Figure 3.23. That's okay; it's a sequence. Keep going. When you pull up more, you reach the end.

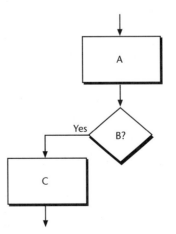

FIGURE 3.23

Now it's time to pull up on the other side of the question. Pull up on the right side. A question pops up (D). See Figure 3.24.

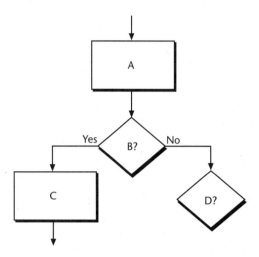

Pull up on the left side of this question. If the line is attached somewhere else, as it is (to step C) in Figure 3.25, just untangle it by repeating the step that is tangled. (In this example, C is repeated to untangle it from the other usage of C.) Keep pulling after C, and you reach the end of the program segment.

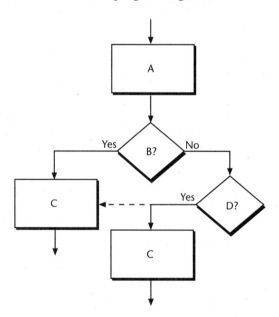

Now pull up on the right side of question D. A process (E) pops up, as shown in Figure 3.26. If you keep pulling, you reach the end.

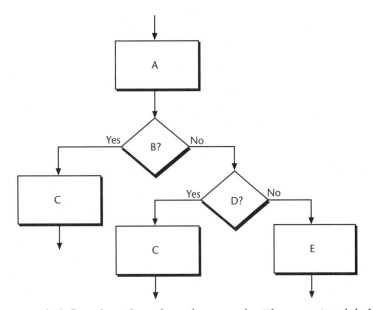

FIGURE 3.26

Now the untangled flowchart has three loose ends. The question labeled D can be brought together to form a selection structure, and then the question B can be brought together to form another selection structure. So you have the flowchart shown in Figure 3.27. The entire flowchart segment is structured—it has a sequence (A) followed by a selection inside a selection.

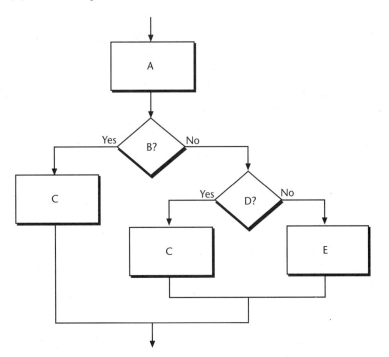

FIGURE 3.27

If you would like to try structuring a very difficult example of an unstructured program, see Appendix A.

Two Special Structures

Any logic problem in the world can be solved using only the three structures: sequence, selection, and loop. However, many programming languages allow two more structures: the case structure and the do until loop. These structures are never *needed* to solve a problem, they are just sometimes more convenient. Programmers would consider them both to be structured.

The Case Structure

The **case structure** is used when there are several distinct possible answers to a question. Suppose you ran a school where tuition was $75, $50, $30, or $10 per credit hour, depending on whether you were a freshman, sophomore, junior, or senior. The structured flowchart in Figure 3.28 shows a series of decisions that you could draw.

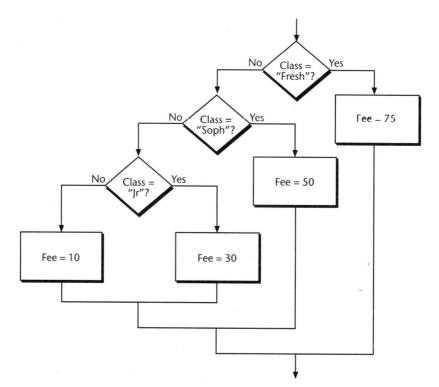

FIGURE 3.28

This logic would be absolutely correct and would be completely structured. The CLASS="JR" selection structure is contained within the CLASS="SOPH" structure, which is contained within the CLASS="FRESH" structure. Note that there is no need to ask if a student is a senior because if a student is not a freshman, sophomore, or junior, it is assumed the student is a senior.

Even though the preceding program segment is correct and structured, many languages would permit a case structure, a flowchart of which is portrayed in Figure 3.29. To many, this program seems easier to read, and since we understand that it *could* be done as a series of structured selections, it is allowed.

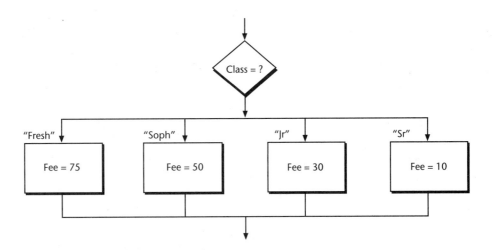

FIGURE 3.29

The Do Until Loop

As you will recall, a structured loop (often called a do while) looks like Figure 3.30. A **do until loop** looks like Figure 3.31.

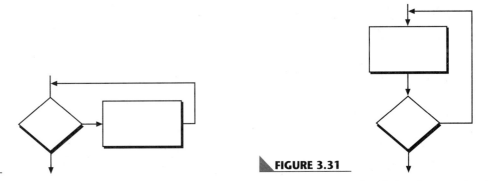

FIGURE 3.30

FIGURE 3.31

There is a big difference between these two structures. In a do while, the question is asked and, depending on the answer, the procedure might never be done. In a do until situation, we want to be sure the procedure is done at least once; then it may or may not be done more times.

The same series of events generated by any do until loop can be guaranteed by having a sequence followed by a do while loop. Consider the flowcharts in Figures 3.32 and 3.33.

sequence & do while

do until

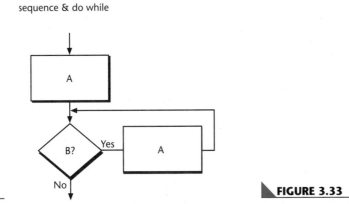

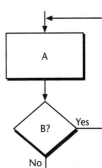

FIGURE 3.32

FIGURE 3.33

In Figure 3.32, A is done, then B is asked. If B is yes, then A is done and B is asked again. Now study Figure 3.33. In Figure 3.33, A is done, then B is asked. If B is yes, then A is done and B is asked again. Both flowcharts do exactly the same thing.

Since we all understand that a do until can be expressed with a sequence followed by a do while, most languages allow the do until.

Pseudocode

Recall from the beginning of Chapter 2 that pseudocode means "false code." Pseudocoding is basically the flowcharting without the boxes. For example, the following pseudocode would be acceptable for the doubling any number of numbers problem:

```
START
      Get NUMBER
      While not EOF
            ANSWER = NUMBER * 2
            Print ANSWER
            Get NUMBER
STOP
```

This book focuses primarily on flowcharting because it is easier for the beginner to keep structured, but pseudocode is very popular and easier to maintain than flowcharts. You may flowchart your first programming problems and switch over to pseudocode when you gain more experience.

TERMS AND CONCEPTS

spaghetti code

structure

sequence

selection (or decision) or if-then-else

null case

loop or repetition or iteration or do while

priming input or priming read

case structure

do until loop

EXERCISES

Exercise 1 **Matching**

Match the term with the structure diagram. (Since the structures go by more than one name, there are more terms than diagrams.)

_____ 1. sequence
_____ 2. selection
_____ 3. loop
_____ 4. do while
_____ 5. do until
_____ 6. decision
_____ 7. if-then-else
_____ 8. iteration

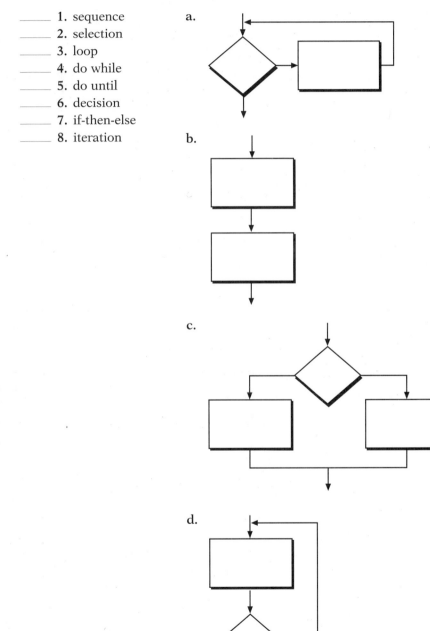

Exercise 2

Is each of the following flowchart segments structured or unstructured? If unstructured, redraw it so it does the same thing but is structured.

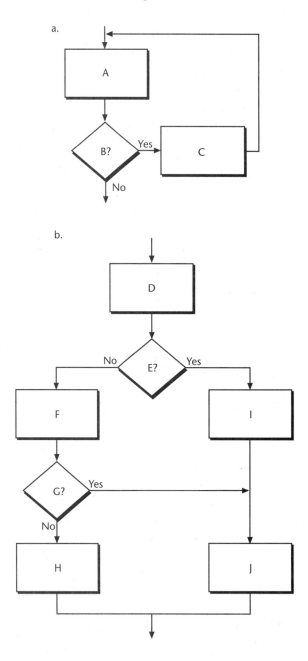

c.

d.

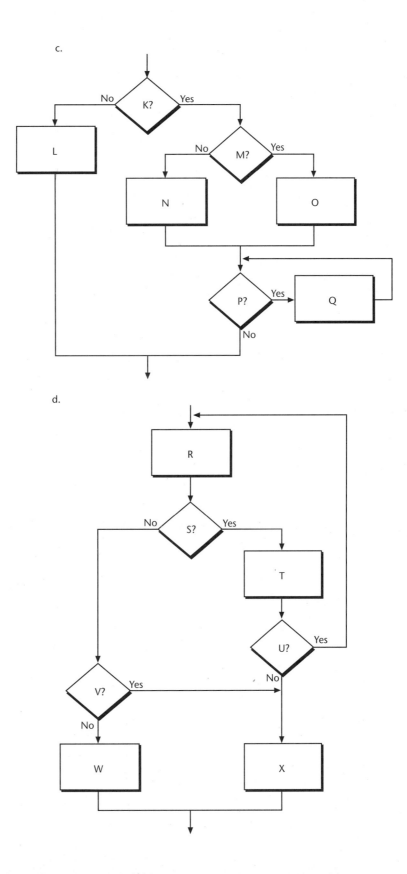

Subroutines and Hierarchy Charts

Objectives

After studying Chapter 4, you should be able to:

- ▶ Describe the uses of subroutines.
- ▶ Explain the difference between local and global variables.
- ▶ Create hierarchy charts.

Subroutines

Programmers seldom write programs as one huge series of steps. Instead, they break the programming problem down into reasonable units and tackle one smaller task at a time. These reasonable units are often called **subroutines**. They also sometimes go by the name **functions** or **procedures**.

The flowcharting symbol for a subroutine is a rectangle with a bar across the top. Inside the rectangle is the name of a subroutine. This book uses the same rule for naming a subroutine as for naming a variable: anything goes as long as it is one word. Therefore a subroutine called DOUBLE-IT might be as indicated in Figure 4.1.

Double-It

FIGURE 4.1

One thing subroutines can do for you is make it easier to see whether or not a program is structured. Figure 4.2 shows our doubling program from Chapter 3 as it was originally written.

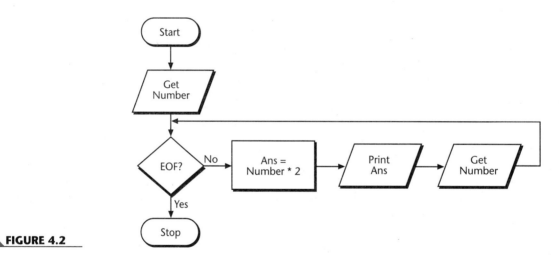

FIGURE 4.2

Figure 4.3 shows the same program calling a subroutine.

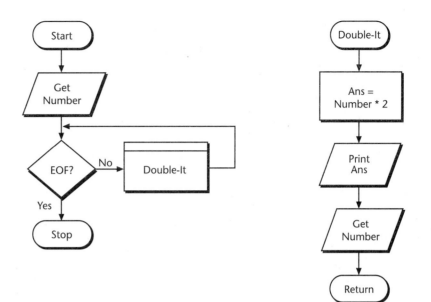

FIGURE 4.3

Both programs do the same thing, and both programs are structured, but the structure may be more obvious in the program with the subroutine because it clearly has a sequence and a loop. The subroutine itself is also clearly just a sequence.

The program with the subroutine works like this:

1. GET NUMBER is executed.
2. EOF is tested.
3. While EOF continues to be false, the DOUBLE-IT subroutine is executed.

> Each time the DOUBLE-IT subroutine is executed, the logic jumps away from the main flowchart and the three steps—ANS = NUMBER * 2, PRINT ANS, and GET NUMBER—are executed sequentially. When the RETURN is encountered in the subroutine, the logic jumps back to the main program, remembering exactly where it left off; that is, ready to test for EOF again.

4. When EOF is no longer false, the program is over.

Of course, seeing whether a program is structured is not the only advantage of having subroutines; in fact it is the least important of the advantages.

Another advantage of using subroutines is the modularity referred to in Chapter 3. Two programmers could be assigned to work on this program at the same time—one to write the main routine or module and the other to write the DOUBLE-IT subroutine or module. Since they each only have to write half the instructions, the whole program can be done in half the time. The subroutine written by one person can then just plug into the calling program.

A third advantage to subroutine use arises when the same steps have to be repeated at several different points in a program. Having a subroutine allows the code to be written once, but the subroutine to be called from different places.

For example, a company might have a file that contains employee data. Some of the data items entered might be NAME, SOC-SEC-NO, BIRTH-MONTH, BIRTH-DAY, BIRTH-YEAR, HIRE-MONTH, HIRE-DAY, HIRE-YEAR, REVIEW-MONTH, REVIEW-DAY, and REVIEW-YEAR. Since the company has had trouble with bad data, that is, mistakes in the file like a HIRE-MONTH of 21, a programmer has been assigned the task of making the program read the file and check the dates entered to make sure that all months fall between 1 and 12 and that all dates are valid for those months. If any date is invalid, an error message is to be printed. This is commonly known as **editing** the data, that is, checking for **reasonableness**. A month of 21 is not reasonable.

Here is part of the programmer's pseudocode:

If BIRTH-MONTH is less than 1 then print "ERROR"
If BIRTH-MONTH is greater than 12 then print "ERROR"
If HIRE-MONTH is less than 1 then print "ERROR"
If HIRE-MONTH is greater than 12 then print "ERROR"
If REVIEW-MONTH is less than 1 then print "ERROR"
If REVIEW-MONTH is greater than 12 then print "ERROR"

Figure 4.4 shows the flowchart for this part of the same program. Notice that the validity checking for BIRTH-MONTH, HIRE-MONTH, and REVIEW-MONTH are similar to each other.

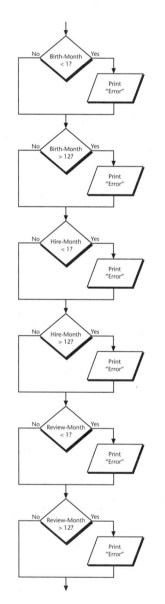

FIGURE 4.4

What if you wrote a subroutine like this:

> *MONTH-ROUTINE*
> *   If WORK-MONTH is less than 1 then print "ERROR"*
> *   If WORK-MONTH is greater than 12 then print "ERROR"*
> *RETURN*

If we declare a field called WORK-MONTH, the main part of the program could be written like this:

> *Move BIRTH-MONTH to WORK-MONTH*
> *Perform MONTH-ROUTINE*
> *Move HIRE-MONTH to WORK-MONTH*
> *Perform MONTH-ROUTINE*
> *Move REVIEW-MONTH to WORK-MONTH*
> *Perform MONTH-ROUTINE*

or flowcharted as shown in Figure 4.5.

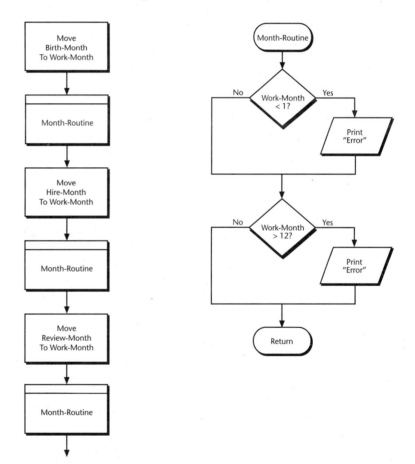

FIGURE 4.5

The same MONTH-ROUTINE is called from three different places in the program. Its tasks are performed three times, but its code has to be written only once. The whole program has a much simpler look.

Of course, the MONTH-ROUTINE could be improved. It could become a DATE-ROUTINE into which more code could be added to determine if the day of the month is higher than 31 for January, 29 for February, and so on. More instructions could even be added to calculate which years are leap years and can have 29 days in February and which years are not and can have only 28, but the program as written will at least find errors in the MONTH part of dates.

Each time the MONTH-ROUTINE subroutine is called, the logic of the program breaks away from the main routine, does the steps in the subroutine, and returns to the next statement after the one it was called from, no matter where that statement may be. All programming languages have this capability of remembering from where their subroutines were called.

Our example had only three months: BIRTH-MONTH, HIRE-MONTH, and REVIEW-MONTH. Imagine if each employee's record also had an INTERVIEW-MONTH, LAST-PROMOTION-MONTH, and PROJECTED-RETIREMENT-MONTH. Former employees would also have a TERMINATION-MONTH in their records. The advantages of writing the month-checking routine only once would skyrocket.

Better still, the company has other files that contain dates—each INVENTORY-RECORD has a MONTH-LAST-ORDERED date and each ACCOUNTS-PAYABLE record has a DUE-MONTH. When programs are modular, one programmer can write one good date-checking routine once, and it can be used in dozens of applications throughout the company.

Local vs. Global Variables

All programming languages can use what are known as **global variables**. They are called global because they can be used throughout the entire program, in the main line logic, or in subroutines. For example, if a simple program is written to give an employee a raise of 100 times her salary, it *could* be written with a subroutine as shown in Figure 4.6.

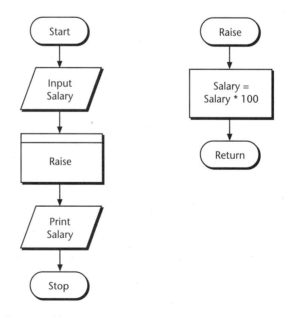

FIGURE 4.6

Remember that the variable name SALARY actually represents a memory location, but because we are working in high-level programming languages, we can give a variable an easy-to-remember name like SALARY.

The variable called SALARY used in the main program is also known to the subroutine called RAISE. SALARY always refers to the same location in computer memory. Because SALARY can be used in any subroutines this program might call, it is known as a global variable.

One disadvantage of global variables is that if two programmers are going to work on writing this program, one programmer writing the main logic and the other writing the RAISE subroutine, the programmers are going to have to agree on the variable name SALARY. If one of the programmers decides to call the variable SALARY and the other decides to call it WAGE, the subroutine will simply not be able to "find" the correct value to multiply.

In some languages, such as Pascal and C, subroutines are called procedures or functions and variables used inside functions *can* be designated as **local variables**. Thus any changes made to variables in these functions or subroutines have no effect on anything outside the routine, unless the programmer takes special action. This is because the main program and each subroutine written use different parts of memory to store their variables. When using local variables, the SALARY variable in the main program would be in a different location from SALARY in the subroutine.

In languages that employ local variables, if the programmer wanted the subroutine to access the SALARY from the main program, the programmer would take the special action of **passing** the SALARY variable to the subroutine. Just how this is done is slightly different for each language, but the result is that the subroutine would get a copy of the value stored in the main program's SALARY to be stored in its own SALARY.

As a matter of fact, the programmer writing the subroutine wouldn't even have to call her variable SALARY. Since a copy of the value is passed to a new *local* memory location for the subroutine to use, the local memory location may be called anything—SALARY, WAGE, RATE, or anything else the programmer chooses.

Languages that work like this may be more confusing than older, more traditional languages that use global variables, but they are highly modular languages because each function can be written with total disregard for any variable names that other programmers may have used in writing other functions. You can add one million to a variable in your subroutine or function without any fear of hurting any variables in anybody else's function unless that programmer specifically passes values to or asks for values back from your function.

If you know you will eventually be coding in a language that uses local variables, you can plan your logic for subroutines without worrying about variable names that might be used by the rest of the program.

For the rest of *this* book, however, I will assume we're planning on a language in which all variables are global, which means they can be changed in value from any spot in the program. If I refer to the SALARY variable in a subroutine, I mean the same SALARY that is referred to in the main logic and all other subroutines of that same program. This will make our examples easier to follow.

Subroutines of Subroutines

Subroutines can also call other subroutines. Recall the MONTH-ROUTINE subroutine from earlier in the chapter. If the subroutine was expanded to check for valid days as well as valid months, we might rename it DATE-ROUTINE and it might look like Figure 4.7.

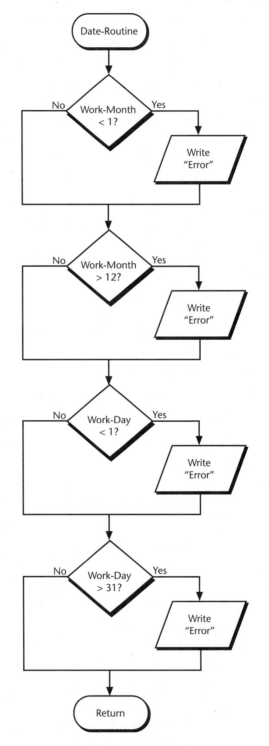

FIGURE 4.7

Although the preceding DATE-ROUTINE works well, it could alternatively be written as shown in Figure 4.8. Then the subroutines that the DATE-ROUTINE calls would be as in Figure 4.9. The main logic now calls DATE-ROUTINE, which calls MONTH-CHECK and DAY-CHECK.

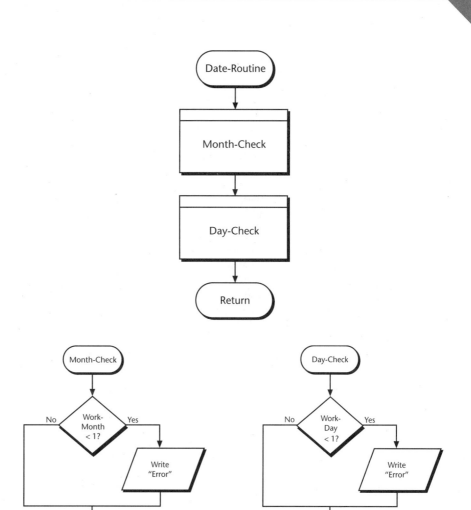

FIGURE 4.8

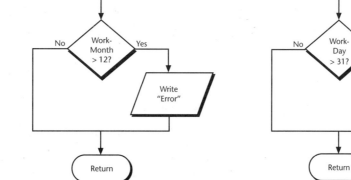

FIGURE 4.9

Both versions of the date-checking program are correct. It is often a matter of programmer style and preference as to exactly what is included in a specific subroutine and how many subroutines there are. There is nothing necessarily better or worse about the main program calling DATE-ROUTINE and DATE-ROUTINE doing all the necessary tasks than there is about DATE-ROUTINE calling two routines of its own, MONTH-CHECK and DAY-CHECK.

Programmers do follow some guidelines when deciding how far to break down subroutines or how much to put in a subroutine. Some places of business may have arbitrary rules such as "a subroutine should never take more than a page" or "a subroutine should never have more than 30 statements in it" or "never have a sub-routine with only one statement in it."

Rather than use such arbitrary rules, a better policy would be to place statements that contribute to one specific task together. The more the statements contribute to the same job, the higher the **functional cohesion** of the subroutine. A routine that checks date validity would be considered cohesive. A routine that checked date validity, deducted insurance premiums, and computed federal withholding tax for an employee would be said to be less cohesive.

Hierarchy Charts

When a program has several subroutines calling other subroutines, programmers often want to use a tool besides flowcharts or pseudocode to show the overall picture of how these subroutines are related to each other. This tool is called a **hierarchy chart**. A hierarchy chart does not tell you what tasks are to be performed within a subroutine; it doesn't tell you *when* or *how* a subroutine is to be performed. It only tells you which routines are in a program and which routines call which other routines.

The hierarchy chart for the last version of the date-checking program would look like Figure 4.10. You can see which routines call which other ones. You don't know *when* the subroutines are called, nor *why* they are called; that information is in the flowchart. A hierarchy chart just tells you subroutines *are* called by other subroutines.

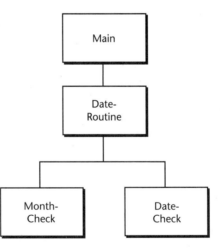

 FIGURE 4.10

Figure 4.11 shows a possible example of a hierarchy chart for the billing program for a mail order company. It provides a general overview of the tasks to be performed without specifying any details.

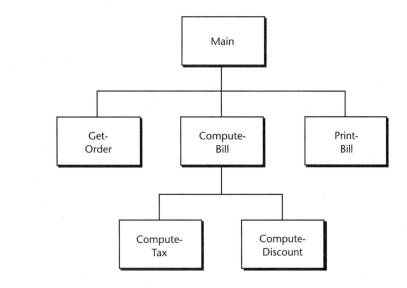

FIGURE 4.11

TERMS AND CONCEPTS

subroutine (function, procedure, module)
editing
reasonableness
local and global variables
passing
functional cohesion
hierarchy chart

XERCISES

ex. *Exercise 1*

Redraw the following flowchart so that the compensation calculations are in a subroutine:

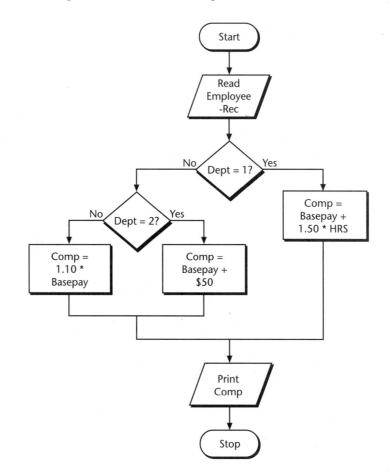

Exercise 2

What are the final values of variables A, B, and C after this program has been run?

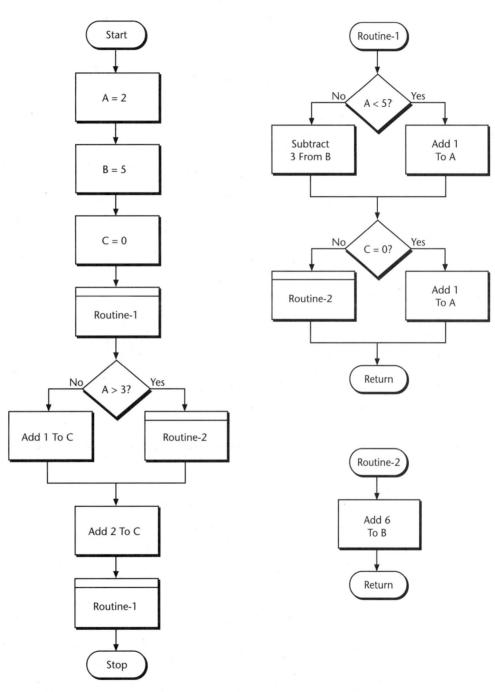

 Exercise 3

Draw a typical hierarchy chart for a paycheck producing program.

Documentation

Objectives

After studying Chapter 5, you should be able to:

▶ Appreciate the need for documentation.
▶ Create a printer spacing chart.

Documentation refers to all of the supporting material that goes along with a program. There are two broad categories of documentation: that which is intended for the programmer and that which is intended for the user.

Program Documentation

Program documentation falls into two categories: **external** and **internal**.

External Program Documentation

External program documentation includes all the supporting paperwork that programmers develop before they write a program. Since most programs have input, processing, and output, external program documentation falls into these categories also.

Output documentation is usually the first to be written. This may seem backwards; but if you're planning a trip, which do you decide first, how to get to your destination or where you're going?

Most requests for programs arise because a user needs particular information to be output, so the planning of program output is usually done in consultation with the person or persons who will be using that output. Only after the desired output is known can the programmer hope to plan the processes needed to produce that output.

The most common type of output is a printed report. The designing of reports is done on **printer spacing charts**, which are also referred to as print charts or print layouts. Basically, this looks like graph paper. The chart has many boxes, and in each box the designer places one character that he or she expects will be printed.

For example, if a report was to be titled INVENTORY REPORT and the user decided this would look best 13 spaces over from the left of the page, the first part of the printer spacing chart would look like Figure 5.1.

```
            INVENTORY REPORT

```

FIGURE 5.1

If it was decided that then a line would be skipped and that the column headings ITEM NAME, PRICE, and QUANTITY IN STOCK were to appear on the report, the printer spacing chart would evolve into Figure 5.2.

```
            INVENTORY REPORT

ITEM NAME   PRICE      QUANTITY IN STOCK

```

FIGURE 5.2

These column headings will be **constant** on every page of the report, so they are written on the print chart literally.

The print layout typically shows how the data will appear on the report. Of course, the data will probably be different every time the report is run. Thus, instead of writing in actual item names and prices, the users and programmers usually use generic X's to represent variable character data and 9's for variable numeric data. (Some programmers use X's for both character and numeric data.) See Figure 5.3.

							I	N	V	E	N	T	O	R	Y		R	E	P	O	R	T							
I	T	E	M		N	A	M	E			P	R	I	C	E				Q	U	A	N	T	I	T	Y		I	N		S	T	O	C	K
X	X	X	X	X	X	X	X	X		9	9	9	.	9	9								9	9	9	9			
X	X	X	X	X	X	X	X	X		9	9	9	.	9	9								9	9	9	9			
X	X	X	X	X	X	X	X	X		9	9	9	.	9	9								9	9	9	9			

▶ **FIGURE 5.3**

Each line, with its X's and 9's representing data, is usually referred to as a **detail line**. Detail lines typically appear many times per page, as opposed to **heading lines**, which usually appear only once per page.

Even though a real inventory report might eventually go on for hundreds or thousands of detail lines, everyone gets the idea after 2 or 3 rows of detail lines. The X's and 9's will represent the data in the same way for every detail line in the report, so there is no need to write any more.

In any report layout then, constant data (like headings) which will be the same on every run of this report, are written in literally, and variable data (like the items, their prices and their quantities), which will change from run to run, are written in X's and 9's.

In our inventory report layout, the headings truly are constant, but you should not assume that all headings are completely constant. Let's say that your user decides to include the date in the preceding report in order to be able to tell one week's report from the next. The report might now have a layout like Figure 5.4. Notice that there is now variable data, the date, in the heading of the report.

		I	N	V	E	N	T	O	R	Y		R	E	P	O	R	T		F	O	R		W	E	E	K		O	F		9	9	/	9	9	/	9	9
I	T	E	M		N	A	M	E			P	R	I	C	E				Q	U	A	N	T	I	T	Y		I	N		S	T	O	C	K
X	X	X	X	X	X	X	X	X		9	9	9	.	9	9								9	9	9	9			
X	X	X	X	X	X	X	X	X		9	9	9	.	9	9								9	9	9	9			
X	X	X	X	X	X	X	X	X		9	9	9	.	9	9								9	9	9	9			

▶ **FIGURE 5.4**

Perhaps, if this is going to be a long report that goes to more than one page, the user will also decide that the headings should appear at the top of every printed page and that page numbers should also be added. See Figure 5.5.

P	9		I	N	V	E	N	T	O	R	Y		R	E	P	O	R	T		F	O	R		W	E	E	K		O	F		9	9	/	9	9	/	9	9
I	T	E	M		N	A	M	E			P	R	I	C	E				Q	U	A	N	T	I	T	Y		I	N		S	T	O	C	K
X	X	X	X	X	X	X	X	X		9	9	9	.	9	9								9	9	9	9			
X	X	X	X	X	X	X	X	X		9	9	9	.	9	9								9	9	9	9			
X	X	X	X	X	X	X	X	X		9	9	9	.	9	9								9	9	9	9			

▶ **FIGURE 5.5**

Just as variable data might appear in a heading, constants might appear in the detail lines. Let's pretend that this company sells everything in dozens. Each number in the QUANTITY IN STOCK column actually represents the number of dozens of that item. The users might choose to see the word DOZEN with each detail line. The print chart in Figure 5.6 indicates that the word DOZEN would literally appear on each line.

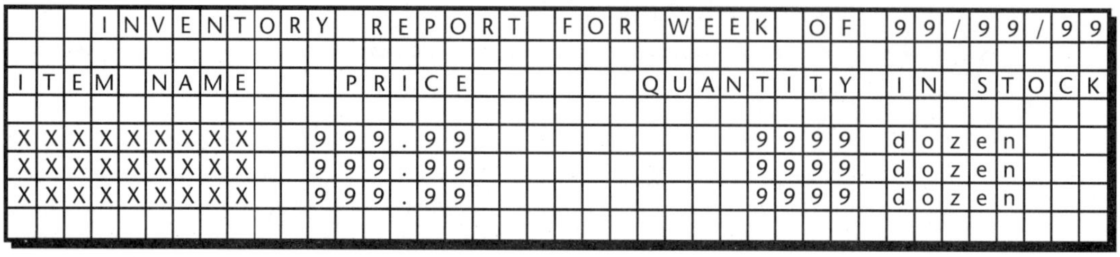

		I	N	V	E	N	T	O	R	Y		R	E	P	O	R	T		F	O	R		W	E	E	K		O	F		9	9	/	9	9	/	9	9	
I	T	E	M		N	A	M	E				P	R	I	C	E						Q	U	A	N	T	I	T	Y		I	N		S	T	O	C	K	
X	X	X	X	X	X	X	X	X		9	9	9	.	9	9									9	9	9	9		d	o	z	e	n	
X	X	X	X	X	X	X	X	X		9	9	9	.	9	9									9	9	9	9		d	o	z	e	n	
X	X	X	X	X	X	X	X	X		9	9	9	.	9	9									9	9	9	9		d	o	z	e	n	

FIGURE 5.6

In the preceding example, most users would probably choose to place the word DOZEN in the heading, something like what is shown in Figure 5.7, thus removing the repetitive constant from the detail lines.

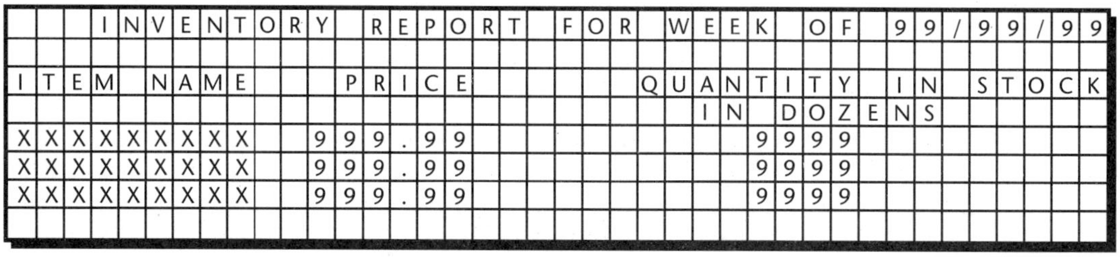

		I	N	V	E	N	T	O	R	Y		R	E	P	O	R	T		F	O	R		W	E	E	K		O	F		9	9	/	9	9	/	9	9
I	T	E	M		N	A	M	E				P	R	I	C	E						Q	U	A	N	T	I	T	Y		I	N		S	T	O	C	K
																					I	N		D	O	Z	E	N	S									
X	X	X	X	X	X	X	X	X		9	9	9	.	9	9									9	9	9	9										
X	X	X	X	X	X	X	X	X		9	9	9	.	9	9									9	9	9	9										
X	X	X	X	X	X	X	X	X		9	9	9	.	9	9									9	9	9	9										

FIGURE 5.7

Besides header lines and detail lines, reports often include special lines at the end of a report. These may have constant data only as in Figure 5.8 or variable data only as in Figure 5.9. Most often, however, reports will have both, as in Figure 5.10.

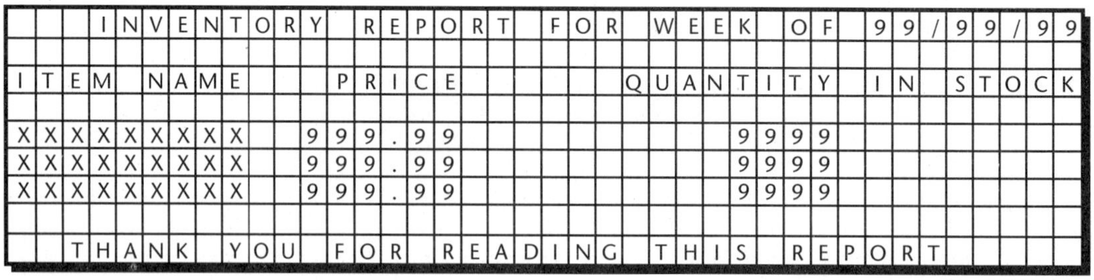

		I	N	V	E	N	T	O	R	Y		R	E	P	O	R	T		F	O	R		W	E	E	K		O	F		9	9	/	9	9	/	9	9
I	T	E	M		N	A	M	E				P	R	I	C	E						Q	U	A	N	T	I	T	Y		I	N		S	T	O	C	K
X	X	X	X	X	X	X	X	X		9	9	9	.	9	9									9	9	9	9										
X	X	X	X	X	X	X	X	X		9	9	9	.	9	9									9	9	9	9										
X	X	X	X	X	X	X	X	X		9	9	9	.	9	9									9	9	9	9										
	T	H	A	N	K		Y	O	U		F	O	R		R	E	A	D	I	N	G		T	H	I	S		R	E	P	O	R	T					

FIGURE 5.8

		I	N	V	E	N	T	O	R	Y		R	E	P	O	R	T		F	O	R		W	E	E	K		O	F		9	9	/	9	9	/	9	9
I	T	E	M		N	A	M	E				P	R	I	C	E						Q	U	A	N	T	I	T	Y		I	N		S	T	O	C	K
X	X	X	X	X	X	X	X	X		9	9	9	.	9	9			.							9	9	9	9									
X	X	X	X	X	X	X	X	X		9	9	9	.	9	9										9	9	9	9									
X	X	X	X	X	X	X	X	X		9	9	9	.	9	9										9	9	9	9									
																									9	9	9	9	9									

FIGURE 5.9

		I	N	V	E	N	T	O	R	Y		R	E	P	O	R	T		F	O	R		W	E	E	K		O	F		9	9	/	9	9	/	9	9
I	T	E	M		N	A	M	E				P	R	I	C	E						Q	U	A	N	T	I	T	Y		I	N		S	T	O	C	K
X	X	X	X	X	X	X	X	X		9	9	9	.	9	9										9	9	9	9									
X	X	X	X	X	X	X	X	X		9	9	9	.	9	9										9	9	9	9									
X	X	X	X	X	X	X	X	X		9	9	9	.	9	9										9	9	9	9									
												T	O	T	A	L		I	N		S	T	O	C	K	9	9	9	9									

FIGURE 5.10

Even though lines at the end of a report don't always contain numeric totals, they are usually referred to generically as **total lines**.

Once the design of the output is planned, the programmer needs to know what input is available to produce this output. Perhaps the programmer will be handed a file description that looks like this:

INVENTORY FILE DESCRIPTION

FILE NAME: INVTRY

FIELD DESCRIPTION	POSITIONS	DATA TYPE	DECIMALS
Name of item	1–15	Character	
Price of item	16–20	Numeric	2
Quantity in stock	21–24	Numeric	0

In addition to these field descriptions, the programmer may be given field names if such variable names must agree with those being used by other programmers working on the project. In many cases, however, the programmer is allowed to choose his or her own variable names.

Recall the relationship of

file
record
field
character

introduced in Chapter 1. The inventory file will have many records, each record with a name of item, price of item, and quantity in stock, which are fields. In turn, for example, the `name of item` field may hold up to 15 characters like "BOLT - 3/4 INCH".

Organizations may use different forms to relay the information about records and fields, but the very least the programmer needs to know is:

1. What is the name of the file?
2. What data does it contain?
3. How much room does the file and each of its fields take up?
4. What type of data is each field—character or numeric?

The preceding inventory file description describes an existing file. It has records stored on it that are 24 characters long. The file's name is INVTRY. The programmer needs to know the file's name in order to be able to access the records it contains.

The first 15 characters are filled with the name of the item. In one record the actual characters might be

"BOLT - 3/4 INCH"

and in the next record they might be

"WHITE GLUE   "

The quotes are not part of the record. They're there to show you the beginning and end of the character field contents. Notice that if an item name does not take up all the allowed spaces, the extra spaces to the right are left blank. This is how character fields are usually stored.

The next several characters in each record of this inventory file are numbers, representing a price. For one record the numbers might be 12345, and for the next record they might be 00025.

The preceding file description indicated that the numeric field holding the price of the item has two decimal places. Therefore, if 12345 is stored in the field, the value represented is 123.45.

When fields in files are supposed to represent dollars and cents, typically no decimal point is stored in the file. If the file holds thousands of records, we would be taking up thousands of positions of storage with decimal places when everybody knows where the decimal place goes anyhow. Programmers say the decimal point is **implied**. 12345 means 123.45 and 00025 means 0.25. Dollar signs and commas are never stored with numeric data either. Dollar signs, commas, or decimal points may be desired on print out and every language has a way for getting them into a report, but they seldom are stored in files used for input.

Notice that if a price does not take up all the allowed spaces, the extra spots to the left are filled with 0's. This is how numeric fields are usually stored.

The last few characters in each record in this inventory file are numbers also. They represent the quantity in stock. The implied decimal figure of 0 means that these numbers are assumed to have no decimal places, that is, they are all whole numbers. Perhaps the value is 3462 on one record and 0009 on another.

The preceding inventory file description appears to have all the data available that would be needed for the inventory report that was designed. But what if this was the inventory file description:

INVENTORY FILE DESCRIPTION

FILE NAME: INVTRY

FIELD DESCRIPTION	POSITIONS	DATA TYPE	DECIMALS
Item number	1–4	Numeric	0
Name of item	5–19	Character	
Cost of item	20–25	Numeric	2
Price of item	26–30	Numeric	2

Quantity in stock	31–34	Numeric	0
Sales rep	35–44	Character	
Sales last year	45–51	Numeric	0

Now, it's harder to see that the information is all there. But it is, and the program can still be written. It's just that some of the fields on input like item number and sales rep will be ignored for the report we want to print. These fields certainly may be used in other reports within the company.

However, if the input file is:

INVENTORY FILE DESCRIPTION

FILE NAME: INVTRY

FIELD DESCRIPTION	POSITIONS	DATA TYPE	DECIMALS
Item number	1–4	Numeric	0
Name of item	5–19	Character	
Cost of item	20–25	Numeric	2
Price of item	26–30	Numeric	2
Sales rep	31–40	Character	
Sales last year	41–47	Numeric	0

then the report can't be printed as designed. If we don't have input data on the quantity in stock, we can't hope to print it on the report. If the user really wants the report, it's out of the programmer's hands until the data can be collected from somewhere.

If the data exists, the program can be written. The programmer can now plan the logic with a flowchart or pseudocode. That is the focus of the rest of this book.

The flowchart or pseudocode should become part of the external program documentation along with any print charts and file layouts. All this material will be useful to the programmer in years to come when revisions must be made to the program.

Internal Program Documentation

After a programmer has planned the logic of a program with a flowchart or pseudocode, the actual code of the program may be written in a programming language. Statements made in programming languages often look cryptic because of the precise syntax required, but at the same time they are also often much shorter than the same statements would be in English. As an example, the instructions:

take the value of the variable AMOUNT and store it in
variables TOTAL and GRAND-TOTAL

can be written in C programming language as

grand_total = total = amount;

Because programming code can be so much more succinct than the English equivalent, and because programming logic can get quite intricate, all programming languages allow for **comments** to be written into programs. The precise manner of accomplishing this varies from language to language: it may be that placing an asterisk in front of a statement or enclosing the statement in brackets makes it a comment. However comments are identified, they are not part of the program that is executed. Instead, they simply allow the programmer to explain in plain English just what the program is doing. Comments will probably prove invaluable to another programmer some day in the future, or even to the original programmer six months in the future when changes need to be made.

User Documentation

After the program is eventually written, tested, and put into production, user documentation also becomes an issue. Are any explanations needed to tell the user how to interpret figures on this report? Are there codes printed that the user needs guidance in understanding? Are any new instructions needed by data entry personnel who will be typing in descriptions and prices of new inventory items in our company? Do the people who operate the computer that will run this program need instructions indicating special paper to be loaded in the printer, or do they need to know how to respond to any prompts that may come up on the computer terminal? All these questions must be taken care of before a program can be said to be fully functional in an organization.

User documentation then includes all the manuals or other instructional materials that nontechnical people use, as well as the operating instructions that computer operators and data entry personnel may need to refer to in the months to come. It needs to be written clearly, in plain language, with reasonable expectations of the users' expertise.

TERMS AND CONCEPTS

documentation

printer spacing chart, print chart, or print layout

internal vs. external documentation

detail lines, heading lines, and total lines

implied decimal point

file description

comments and programmer documentation

user documentation

representation of constant vs. variable data

EXERCISES

 Exercise 1

Design a print chart for a payroll roster that is intended to list for every employee: employee's first name, last name, and salary.

 Exercise 2

Design a print chart for a payroll roster that is intended to list for every employee: employee's first name, last name, hours worked, rate per hour, gross pay, federal withholding tax, state withholding tax, union dues, and net pay.

Exercise 3

Given this input file description:

INSURANCE PREMIUM LIST

FILE NAME: INSPREM

FIELD DESCRIPTION	POSITIONS	DATA TYPE	DECIMALS
Name of insured	1–40	Character	
Birth date	41	Numeric	0
Gender	42	Character	
Make of car	43–52	Character	
Year of car	53–54	Numeric	0
Miles per year	55–60	Numeric	0
Number of tickets	61–62	Numeric	0

determine if there is enough information given to produce each of these reports:

a. A list of the names of all insured drivers.

b. A list of very high risk drivers defined as those who are male, under 25, with more than 2 tickets.

c. A list of low risk drivers defined as those with no tickets in the last 3 years, over 30 years old.

d. A list of drivers to contact about a special premium offer for those with a passenger car who drive under 10,000 miles per year.

A Complete Program

Objectives

After studying Chapter 6, you should be able to:

▶ Draw the logic of a complete computer program.

▶ Describe the functions of housekeeping routines, main loops, and closing routines.

▶ Explain the concept of opening and closing files.

You're ready for your first programming challenge! Your boss has decided on the output:

						I	N	V	E	N	T	O	R	Y		R	E	P	O	R	T									
I	T	E	M		N	A	M	E			P	R	I	C	E					Q	U	A	N	T	I	T	Y		I	N		S	T	O	C	K
X	X	X	X	X	X	X	X	X	X		9	9	9	.	9	9													9	9	9	9				
X	X	X	X	X	X	X	X	X	X		9	9	9	.	9	9													9	9	9	9				

You have been provided with the input description:

INVENTORY FILE DESCRIPTION

FILE NAME: INVEN

FIELD CONTENTS	POSITIONS	DATA TYPE	DECIMALS
Item name	1–15	Character	
Price	16–20	Numeric	2
Quantity in stock	21–24	Numeric	0

Since you know *all* about flowcharting and structure, you're ready to go.

Getting started is the hardest part. Where should you begin? It's wisest to try to get the big picture first. Almost every program that exists in the world follows this general format:

1. **Housekeeping**, or **initialization**—the steps that are done to set everything up at the beginning.
2. **Main loop of the program**—the steps that are done over and over again for every record in a file until the end of the file (EOF) has been reached.
3. **End-of-job routine**—the steps that are done after the last record has been read.

The main flowchart of many programs, therefore, can be broken down into three major subroutines, as shown in Figure 6.1. The subroutine names, of course, are entirely up to the programmer.

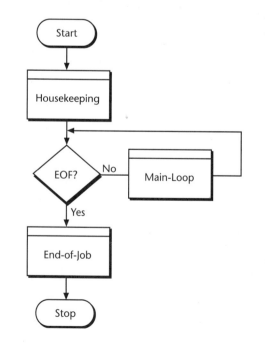

FIGURE 6.1

The hierarchy chart, then, would be as shown in Figure 6.2.

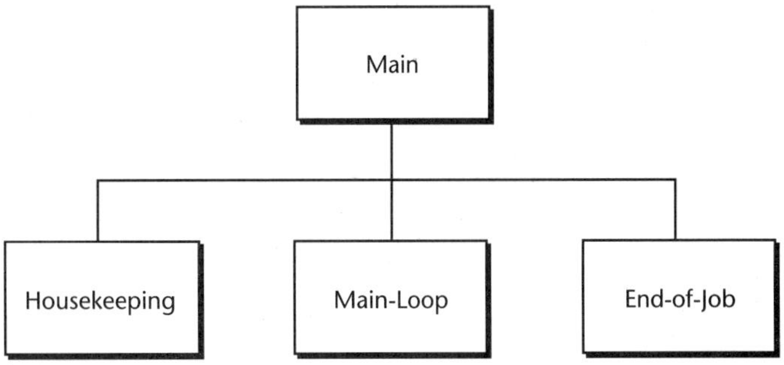

FIGURE 6.2

Breaking down a big program into three or so basic procedures helps keep the job manageable, allowing you to tackle it one step at a time. It allows you to assign the three major procedures to three different programmers, if you so desire. It also helps you to keep the program structured.

Housekeeping

What needs to happen in the HOUSEKEEPING routine? Very often, four major tasks need to be performed:

1. Variables need to be **created**, also known as **defining** or **declaring** them.

   How variables are set up in memory depends on the programming language you will use, but, at the very least, variables need to be named. Some variables may also need to be **initialized**, that is, set to specific starting values. A variable to be used to count things might be set at 0; a variable to be used to hold a heading might be set to the characters "INVENTORY REPORT".

2. Files need to be opened.

   If a program will use input files, the computer must be told where the input is coming from—a specific disk drive, for example, or a tape drive. Since a disk may have many files stored on it, the program also needs to know the name of the file being opened for use. In many languages, if no input file is opened, input is accepted from a default device, most often the keyboard.

   If a program will have output, a file for output must be opened also. Perhaps this is the printer or maybe a disk or tape drive. Again, if no file is opened, a default device, usually the monitor, is used.

3. Other tasks that happen only at the beginning of a program need to be performed.

   In our inventory example, if we assume that the report will never be more than one page long, and if we know we want to print the headings indicated on the print layout chart at the top of a page, the headings could be written during the HOUSEKEEPING subroutine.

4. The first record needs to be read from the input file.

   This is necessary for at least two good reasons. Recall the main logic of our program (see Figure 6.1).

When HOUSEKEEPING is finished, the program immediately checks for EOF. This makes sense if the last HOUSEKEEPING step is to read a record from the input file. If EOF is not encountered, there must be a legitimate record to be processed and we enter the MAIN-LOOP of the program. If, however, EOF is encountered, there is no point in entering the MAIN-LOOP; we may as well go straight to the END-OF-JOB routine.

If HOUSEKEEPING did not include a step to read a record from the input file, then the first MAIN-LOOP step would have to be to read a record. The program would work well until it encountered EOF, but then the MAIN-LOOP record processing would continue without any data to process. (If the reasoning for the READ statement at the end of HOUSEKEEPING still eludes you, reread the section about the priming read in Chapter 3.) The HOUSEKEEPING routine for the inventory program then could look like Figure 6.3.

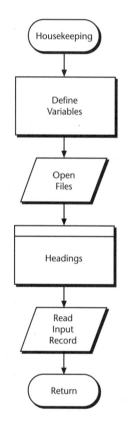

FIGURE 6.3

Let's look at a few vague things about this subroutine. For one thing, DEFINE VARIABLES doesn't tell us anything about the variables being defined. This book uses the convention of adding an annotation symbol to flowcharts, as shown in Figure 6.4. The annotation symbol gives you room to expand on anything written in a flowchart box that may not be complete enough.

FIGURE 6.4

One set of variable names that needs to be created for the inventory program is the names to be used to refer to the fields in the input file. The fields that hold the item description, the price, and the quantity in stock can be referred to by any names the programmer chooses as long as they follow the variable naming rules set up in Chapter 2:

1. Variable names are one word.

2. Variable names have meaning.

Therefore, the variable that holds the name of an item could be ITEM-NAME; one that holds the price of an item could be PRICE, and quantity in stock could be QUANTITY. (See Figure 6.5).

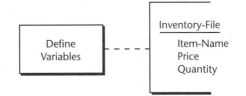

FIGURE 6.5

This book also uses the convention of grouping fields on the input file together so they can be easily identified as input. They will have a group name, like INVENTORY-FILE, which will be underlined. Indented underneath the group name will be a list of the individual field names.

Fields in input files never need to be initialized to any values. It would be meaningless to say ITEM-NAME = "BOLT - 3/4 INCH" for several reasons.

First of all, ITEM-NAME is going to be equal to many different values during the execution of this program. If 30 items exist on the inventory file, ITEM-NAME will eventually have had 30 different values.

Second, "BOLT - 3/4 INCH" may be one of our inventory items now, but it may not be a year from now. Inventory item names are going to be read off of an input file and they are going to be whatever is on the file at any point in the future.

Third, even if ITEM-NAME is set equal to some value, that value will be wiped out the first time a record is read from the input file. Whatever the name is for the first item on the file will be placed into the memory spot ITEM-NAME, and whatever used to be there will be completely wiped out.

Another variable I might want to create in my inventory program is a heading to print "INVENTORY REPORT" at the top of the page. This area should be initialized. The heading is always going to be "INVENTORY REPORT," and it's not going to change no matter how many inventory records are read from the input file. In some languages, a field that is never going to change is called a **constant**. Such a field might be as shown in Figure 6.6. A second heading line with the words "ITEM NAME PRICE   QUANTITY IN STOCK" could be indicated as in Figure 6.7.

FIGURE 6.6, 6.7

Heading lines that print in the format

INVENTORY REPORT

ITEM NAME   PRICE   QUANTITY IN STOCK

must be defined as two separate lines because printers print one full line at a time. Therefore, one of these lines is eventually sent to the printer, then the other one.

The variable names HEADING-1 and HEADING-2 are entirely up to the programmer. You may have preferred HEAD-ONE and HEAD-TWO or FIRST-TITLE and SECOND-TITLE or MAIN-HEAD and COLUMN-HEADS. As long as you follow the two rules—variable names are one word and have meaning—the actual names are a matter of individual choice.

The completed HOUSEKEEPING now looks like Figure 6.8.

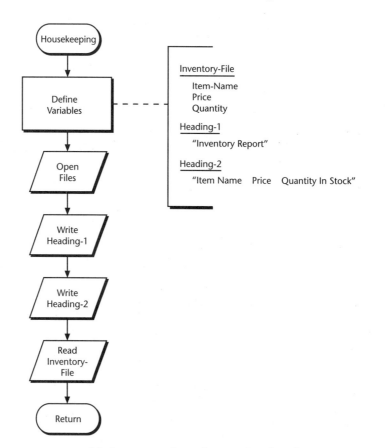

FIGURE 6.8

Some programmers would choose to place the two heading line statements in their own subroutine. Therefore, HOUSEKEEPING would be as shown in Figure 6.9, with the steps in HEADINGS appearing as in Figure 6.10. Either approach would be fine.

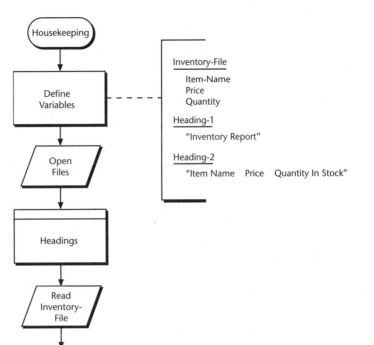

FIGURE 6.9

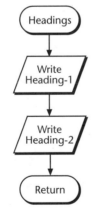

FIGURE 6.10

MAIN-LOOP

The MAIN-LOOP of this program is not complicated. There is no math to be done and there are no decisions to be made in this inventory program. After the first record is read in from the input file in HOUSEKEEPING, if EOF was not encountered, MAIN-LOOP is entered and each of the fields from the input record is written as a part of the detail line. Figure 6.11 shows this step.

FIGURE 6.11

Just as headings are printed one full line at a time, detail lines are also printed one line at a time. In some languages, the statement that would write one detail line for the inventory report would simply be

write ITEM-NAME, PRICE, QUANTITY

just as is indicated in the flowchart. In other languages, we would be more likely to set up a work area in which to place each of the fields that will be written for one record. Only when the line is filled up with information will it be printed.

The simpler approach, naming the fields to be printed, will be used here. This book assumes that one WRITE statement produces one line of output. The flowchart segment in Figure 6.12 shows the printing of three *separate* lines, one below the other. Since that is *not* what we want according to the designed print chart, it is *not* how the flowchart will be drawn.

FIGURE 6.12

After the detail line has been written, one last step needs to be taken before leaving the MAIN-LOOP. A new inventory record is read into memory from the input file. When MAIN-LOOP is exited, the logic goes to the EOF question. If it is not EOF, the MAIN-LOOP is entered again, the detail from the second record is printed, and the third record is read into memory.

During some execution of the MAIN-LOOP, when reading a new record, EOF will be encountered. Then, when the EOF question is asked in the main line of the program, the answer will be yes, and the MAIN-LOOP will not be entered again. Instead, the END-OF-JOB routine will be entered.

The complete MAIN-LOOP, then, is as shown in Figure 6.13.

FIGURE 6.13

END-OF-JOB

For this inventory report program, the END-OF-JOB routine is very simple. No "Thank you for reading this report" lines are indicated on the print layout chart; there are no total lines. Nothing special happens. Only one task needs to be performed. In HOUSEKEEPING, we opened files. In END-OF-JOB, we always close them. The complete END-OF-JOB routine, then, is as shown in Figure 6.14.

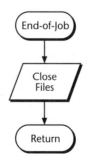

FIGURE 6.14

Most programmers wouldn't bother with a subroutine for just one statement, but soon our end-of-job routines will get bigger and more complicated and it will make more sense to see them together in a subroutine.

In some languages, like COBOL, a read statement and an EOF? question cannot be in separate subroutines as I have them here (READ is in MAIN-LOOP, but EOF? is in the main line of the program.) Therefore, many programmers would code the final steps in both HOUSEKEEPING and MAIN-LOOP to not only read a record, but to immediately check for EOF also. See Figure 6.15.

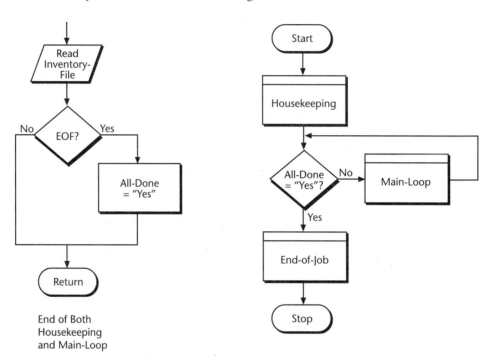

FIGURE 6.15

End of Both
Housekeeping
and Main-Loop

After each read statement, if EOF is encountered, some **flag**, a variable named something like ALL-DONE, will be set to "YES." Then the main line of the program would check for ALL-DONE equal to "YES." If it isn't, MAIN-LOOP will be entered; if it is, END-OF-JOB will be entered.

Of course, it is the programmer's responsibility to make sure ALL-DONE is something other than "YES" when the program begins, perhaps by initializing it to anything but "YES" in the HOUSEKEEPING routine.

TERMS AND CONCEPTS

housekeeping (initialization)

main loop

end-of-job routine

creating, defining, or declaring variables

initializing variables

opening and closing of files

flag

EXERCISES

 ## *Exercise 1*

A pet store wishes to produce a weekly sales report. The output consists of a printed report entitled PET SALES. Fields printed on output are: type of animal and sale price. You have been provided with the following input description:

PET FILE DESCRIPTION

FILE NAME: PETS

FIELD CONTENTS	POSITIONS	DATA TYPE	DECIMALS
Type of Animal	1–20	Character	
Price	21–24	Numeric	2

Design the print chart, draw the hierarchy chart, and draw the flowchart for this program.

 ## *Exercise 2*

An employer wishes to produce a personnel report. The output consists of a printed report entitled ACTIVE PERSONNEL. Fields printed on output are: last name of employee, first name of employee, and current salary. You have been provided with the following input description:

PERSONNEL FILE DESCRIPTION

FILE NAME: PERSONNL

FIELD CONTENTS	POSITIONS	DATA TYPE	DECIMALS
Last name	1–15	Character	
First name	16–30	Character	
Soc. sec. number	31–39	Numeric	0
Department	40–41	Numeric	0
Salary	42–45	Numeric	

Design the print chart, draw the hierarchy chart, and draw the flowchart for this program.

 ## *Exercise 3*

An employer wishes to produce a personnel report that shows the end result if he gives everyone a 10% raise in salary. The output consists of a printed report entitled PROJECTED RAISES. Fields printed on output are: last name of employee, first name of employee, current salary, and projected salary. You have been provided with the following input description:

PERSONNEL FILE DESCRIPTION

FILE NAME: PERSONNL

FIELD CONTENTS	POSITIONS	DATA TYPE	DECIMALS
Last name	1–15	Character	
First name	16–30	Character	
Soc. sec. number	31–39	Numeric	0
Department	40–41	Numeric	0
Salary	42–45	Numeric	

Design the print chart, draw the hierarchy chart, and draw the flowchart for this program.

Decision Making

Objectives

After studying Chapter 7, you should be able to:

- ▶ Better understand the decision structure.
- ▶ Flowchart nested decisions.
- ▶ Explain the differences between AND and OR logic.

The reason people think computers are smart lies in the computer program's ability to make decisions. A medical diagnosis program that can decide if your symptoms fit various disease profiles seems quite intelligent, as does a program that can offer you different potential vacation routes based on your destination.

The **decision structure** is not new to you—it's one of the basic structures of structured programming. See Figure 7.1.

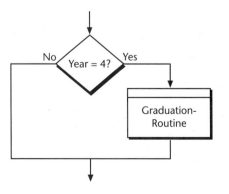

FIGURE 7.1

Some programmers might refer to the structure in Figure 7.1 as a **dual-alternative decision** or an **if-then-else** because it fits the statement:

IF the answer to the question is yes THEN do something ELSE do the something else.

For example, consider Figure 7.2.

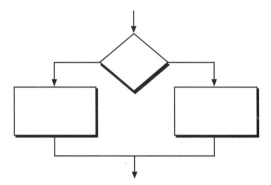

FIGURE 7.2

A special case of the if-then-else is the **single-alternative decision** or an **if-then**, as in

IF the answer to the question is yes THEN do something.

For example, consider Figure 7.3.

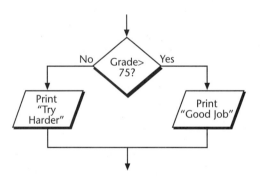

FIGURE 7.3

The single-alternative decision could always be expressed as a dual-alternative decision as shown in Figure 7.4, but if a symbol is going to indicate that you have to do nothing, most programmers would not bother with that symbol.

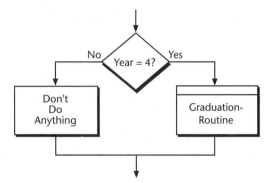

FIGURE 7.4

Almost always, a question can be asked in at least two ways. For example, a payroll program often computes overtime if a worker has put in more than 40 hours. The OVERTIME routine may be called if HOURS are more than 40, or if HOURS are *not* less than or equal to 40. The two flowchart segments in Figure 7.5 have identical results. Of these two subroutines, neither is better or worse. It is up to the programmer to use the decision structure that makes more sense to him or her.

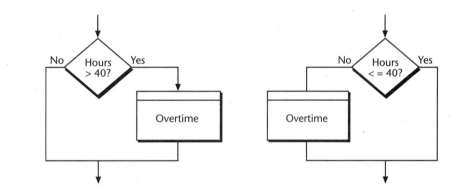

FIGURE 7.5

The AND Situation

In programs, very often, more than one decision is needed to determine whether something is to be done. For example, suppose that an employee who works over 40 hours gets overtime pay only if he or she is a class 1 worker. Perhaps class 2 workers are salaried and do not get overtime. Perhaps class 3 workers are contractual and do not get overtime either.

This type of situation is known as an **AND** situation because the employee's record must pass two tests—have hours greater than 40 *and* class equal to 1—before that employee can get overtime. An AND situation requires a **nested decision** or a **nested if**, that is, a decision "inside of" another decision.

The flowchart can be expressed like this:

IF the employee works over 40 hours, THEN and ONLY THEN, test to see if the employee is a class 1 employee; if so, THEN AND ONLY THEN compute overtime.

and illustrated as in Figure 7.6.

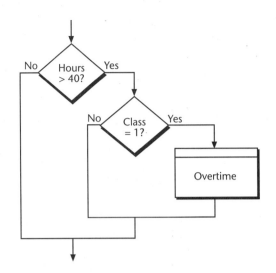

FIGURE 7.6

The flowchart could also be expressed like this:

> *IF the employee is a class 1 employee, THEN and ONLY THEN, test to see if the employee has worked over 40 hours.*

and illustrated as in Figure 7.7.

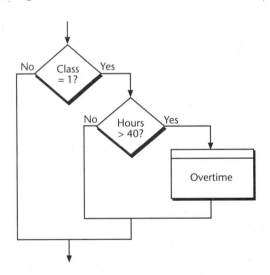

FIGURE 7.7

Does it make a difference which question is asked first? As far as the output goes, no. In both flowchart segments, any employee working 40 hours or fewer will not get overtime. In both flowchart segments, any employee not in class 1 will not get overtime. In both flowchart segments, an employee would have to work over 40 hours *and* be in class 1 to enter the OVERTIME routine.

As far as program efficiency goes, however, it may make a difference which question is asked first. Let's pretend that out of 1000 employees in our company, about half, or 500, are class 1 workers. Let's also pretend that out of 1000 employees, only about 10% or 100 put in overtime in any given week. Now look at the two flowchart segments.

If we have 1000 employees and if the first question asked is the question about the hours, this question will be asked 1000 times. For 90% of our employees, or 900 of the records, the answer is no, they have not worked over 40 hours. For only 100 employees do we need to ask the question about class. About half the 100 will be class 1 employees, so about 50 records will enter the OVERTIME subroutine. For 50 employees, overtime will be calculated, and we had to ask 1100 questions to find them. See Figure 7.8.

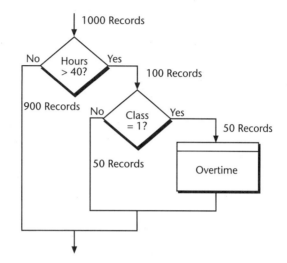

FIGURE 7.8

If we ask the class question first, we ask that question 1000 times. About half the employees are class 1 employees, so for 500 people we're done. On the remaining 500, however, the question of hours worked needs to be asked. About 10% of these employees will have worked over 40 hours, so about 50 of them will enter the OVERTIME routine. These are the same 50 employees as in the preceding routine, but it has taken 1500 questions to find them. See Figure 7.9.

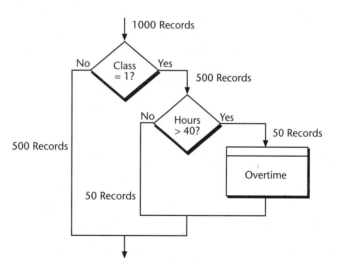

FIGURE 7.9

The 400-question difference between the first flowchart and the second flowchart really will not take much time on most computers. But, it will take some time, and if there are hundreds of thousands of employees instead of only 1000, or if many such decisions have to be made within a program, performance time can be significantly improved by asking questions in the proper order.

In many situations, the programmer has no idea which of two events is most likely to occur; in that case, either question may legitimately be asked first. In general, however, in AND situations, if probabilities are known, the question that is *least likely* to cause an event to happen should be asked first, in order to eliminate as many records as possible from having to go through the second decision.

A common programming mistake for new programmers would be to code the overtime program for class 1 employees as shown in Figure 7.10. In this diagram both questions are asked, and the question least likely to cause overtime is asked first, but the logic is wrong.

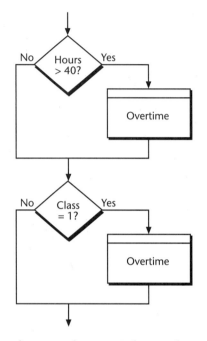

FIGURE 7.10

In this flowchart, if an employee works over 40 hours, the OVERTIME routine is performed even though the employee is a class 2 or 3 employee. If an employee is class 1, the overtime routine is performed even if the employee didn't work over 40 hours. Still worse, if an employee is in class 1 and works over 40 hours, the OVERTIME routine is performed *twice*. This flowchart is incorrect for this program.

The OR Decision

Sometimes a routine is to be performed when one or the other of two conditions is true. This is called an OR situation because either one condition must be met *or* some other condition must be met in order for some event to take place.

For example, let's say an employer is going to give a bonus to all class 1 and class 2 employees. Let's say the bonus is calculated in a subroutine called BONUS. Then a flowchart segment to do this might look like Figure 7.11.

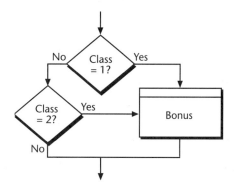

FIGURE 7.11

If you follow this flowchart, you can see that if an employee is in class 1, that employee's record will enter the BONUS routine. If the employee is not in class 1 but is in class 2, the employee will enter the BONUS routine. The employee gets a bonus if he or she is in class 1 *or* class 2. So what's wrong with the flowchart? It's not structured!

The rules of structure say a decision must look like Figure 7.12.

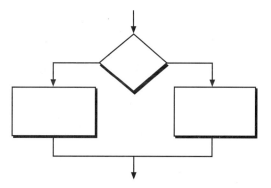

FIGURE 7.12

There must be one entry to and one exit from the structure, and any decision must be completed by the joining of its two branches at the bottom.

How do we straighten out the BONUS subroutine? Why not use the "spaghetti bowl" method from Chapter 3? Start at the top of the subroutine. There is a question, which is going to be the beginning of a decision structure. See Figure 7.13.

FIGURE 7.13

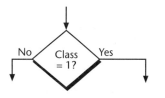

Tugging on the right string, a box pops up (BONUS) and the end of the routine is reached. See Figure 7.14.

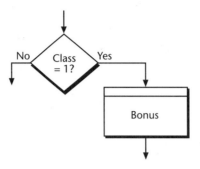

FIGURE 7.14

Now pull on the left side of the decision. A new question pops up—the beginning of a new decision structure. See Figure 7.15.

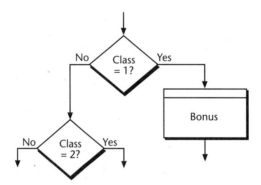

FIGURE 7.15

Pull on its right side, untangling any lines and repeating any procedures that need to be repeated to get to the bottom. We end up repeating the BONUS routine, and then we reach the end. See Figure 7.16.

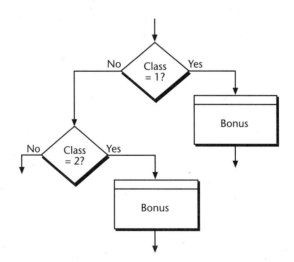

FIGURE 7.16

Pull on the left side of the decision. That's simple; we have reached the end. See Figure 7.17.

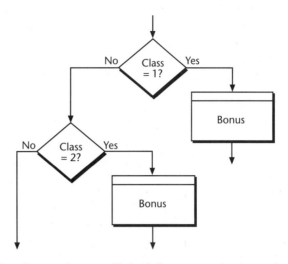

FIGURE 7.17

There are three dangling ends, so pull the left two together to make a complete decision structure. See Figure 7.18.

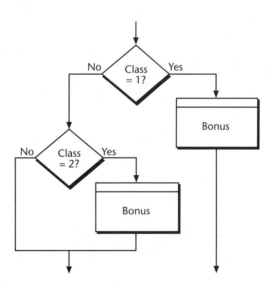

FIGURE 7.18

Now pull the remaining two ends together, and you have a decision structure within a decision structure. The whole thing is structured! It's a nested decision.

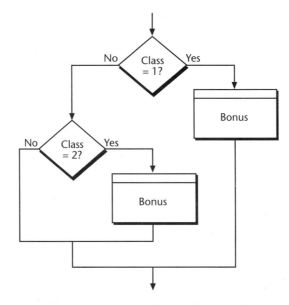

FIGURE 7.19

Actually, there are two different ways to configure the nested decision that dispenses a bonus to people who are class 1 or class 2 employees. If you examine the flowchart segments in Figures 7.19 and 7.20, you will see that both perform the BONUS routine for any employee who is in class 1 or in class 2.

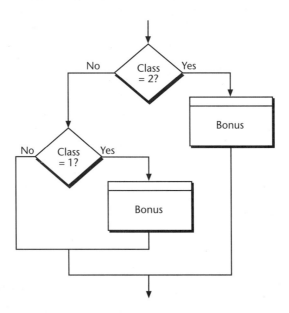

FIGURE 7.20

Which subroutine is better? As you might have guessed, it depends on the probabilities of employees being in class 1, class 2, or some other class. Of course, the programmer may have no idea which class is most common. However, let's hypothetically say that of 1000 employees you know, 50% are class 1, 30% are class 2, and 20% are class 3.

If you ask whether an employee is in class 1 first, 1000 questions are asked. About 50%, or 500, pass the test and go to the BONUS routine. For the other 500, a second question is asked: Is the employee in class 2? About 300 of these employees will be in class 2, and their records will go to the BONUS routine. The other 200 employees will pass out of this routine without ever making it to the BONUS routine. In the end, 1500 questions were asked and 800 bonuses were calculated. See Figure 7.21.

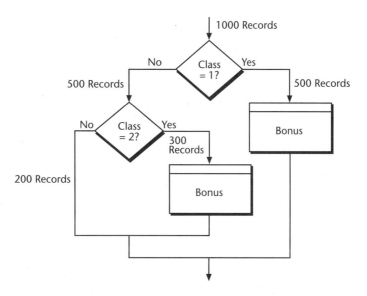

FIGURE 7.21

On the other hand, if the class 2 question is asked first, 1000 questions are asked and about 300 pass the test and go on to the BONUS routine. The other 700 need to have the question about class 1 asked. Of these, 500 are in class 1 and go to the BONUS routine. Again, 800 bonuses are calculated, but this time 1700 questions had to be asked instead of 1500. See Figure 7.22.

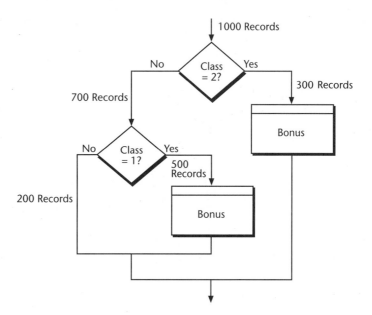

FIGURE 7.22

The general rule on OR situations then is to ask the question first that is *most* likely to cause an event to occur. This is because the process will be performed on either of two conditions, so by asking the more frequently occurring condition first, you go ahead and do the process, not bothering with the second question for many of the records.

Actually, a clever programmer would not use an OR situation for the preceding scenario at all. A clever programmer would conclude that if employees in classes 1 and 2 were getting bonuses and employees in class 3 were not, the quickest approach would be to simply ask if an employee is in class 3. If not, perform the BONUS routine. This approach requires only 1000 decisions for 1000 records and is the fastest solution of all. See Figure 7.23.

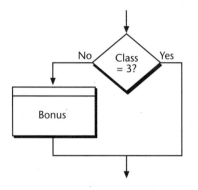

FIGURE 7.23

Of course, if there were many classes, like 0, 3, 4, and 5, that did *not* receive a bonus, it would again become more efficient to ask if class was equal to 1 or 2.

Combined Decisions

Many modern programming languages allow the programmer to ask two questions at once. See Figure 7.24.

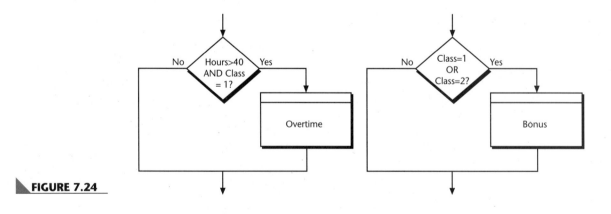

FIGURE 7.24

Even though you may be working with a language that allows this syntax, the computer actually makes only one decision at a time. The order in which the two parts of the question are asked may still affect the running time of the program. Therefore, even if you are programming in a language that allows two questions in one statement, it may be important to ask the two parts of the question in the right order.

TERMS AND CONCEPTS

nested decision
AND situation
OR situation
dual-alternative decision
if-then-else
single-alternative decision
if-then

EXERCISES

 Exercise 1

For a carpenter, draw the logic that would compute the price of a desk based on the following input fields: LENGTH-IN-INCHES, WIDTH-IN-INCHES, WOOD, DRAWERS. The price is computed as follows:

- All desks are a minimum $200.
- If the surface (length * width) is over 750 square inches, a $50 charge is added.
- If the wood is "mahogany," a $150 charge is added; for "oak" a $125 charge is added. No charge is added for "pine."
- An additional $30 is charged for every drawer in the desk.

Exercise 2

A nursery maintains a file of all plants in stock along with such data as price and characteristics. It is known that only 20% of the nursery stock does well in shade and 50% of the nursery stock does well in sandy soil. Draw the flowchart segment that would perform the most efficient search for a plant for a shady, sandy yard.

Exercise 3

A company is attempting to organize carpools to save energy. Ten percent of the company's employees live in Wonder Lake. Thirty percent of the employees live in Woodstock. Since these towns are both north of the company, the company wants a list of employees who live in either town so it can recommend that these employees drive in together. Draw the most efficient process for selecting these employees, assuming there is a field called CITY in each employee's personnel record.

Exercise 4

A supervisor in a manufacturing company wishes to produce a report showing which employees have increased their production this month over last month so that she can issue them a certificate of commendation. She wishes to have a report with three columns: last name, first name, and the either the word "UP" or blanks printed under the column heading PRODUCTION. "UP" gets printed when this year's production is a greater number than last year's production. Input exists as follows:

PRODUCTION FILE

FILE NAME: PRODUCTN

FIELD CONTENTS	POSITIONS	DATA TYPE	DECIMALS
Last name	1–20	Character	
First name	21–30	Character	
Last year's production	31–34	Numeric	0
This year's production	35–38	Numeric	0

Create the print layout chart, hierarchy chart, and flowchart for this program.

 Exercise 5

A supervisor in a manufacturing company wishes to produce a report showing bonuses she is planning to give based on this year's production. She wishes to have a report with three columns: last name, first name, and bonus. Input exists as follows:

PRODUCTION FILE

FILE NAME: PRODUCTN

FIELD CONTENTS	POSITIONS	DATA TYPE	DECIMALS
Last name	1–20	Character	
First name	21–30	Character	
Last year's production	31–34	Numeric	0
This year's production	35–38	Numeric	0

The bonuses will be distributed as follows:

This Year's Production	Bonus
1000 units and under	$25
1001 to 3000 units	$50
3001 to 6000 units	$100
6001 units and up	$200

Create the print layout chart, hierarchy chart, and flowchart for this program.

Exercise 6

Modify Exercise 5 to reflect these new facts and have the program execute as efficiently as possible:

- Bonuses will only be given to those whose production this year is higher than last year. This is true for approximately 30% of the employees.
- 75% of employees produce over 6000 units per year, only 5% produce under 1000.

Looping

Objectives

After studying Chapter 8, you should be able to:

▶ Better understand the loop structure.
▶ Flowchart looping logic.

If making decisions is what makes computers seem intelligent, it's looping that makes computers worthwhile.

Consider the following set of instructions for a typical payroll program:

1. Get employee-record (with hours, rate, and so on).
2. Multiply first 40 hours by rate giving regular pay.
3. If hours > 40, multiply (hours – 40) by rate by 1.5 giving overtime.
4. Add regular and overtime giving gross.
5. Determine federal withholding tax based on gross and dependents.
6. Determine state tax based on gross, dependents, and state of residence.
7. Determine insurance deduction based on code.
8. Determine social security based on gross.
9. Subtract federal tax, state tax, social security and insurance from gross.

.
.
.

In reality, this list is too short—companies deduct stock option plans, charitable contributions, union dues, and other items from checks in addition to the items mentioned in this list. Sometimes they also pay bonuses and commissions. Sick days and vacation days are taken into account and handled appropriately. As you can see, payroll programs are complicated.

The beauty of having a computer is that all of the preceding instructions need to be figured out *only once*. Then the instructions can be repeated over and over again using a **loop**, specifically a do-while structure.

The Do-While

Recall the loop or do-while structure. (See Figure 8.1) Chapter 6 explained that almost every useful program has a **main loop**. A few housekeeping tasks are performed at the start of the program, and a few clean-up tasks are performed at the end, but most of the tasks of a program are repeated over and over for many (sometimes hundreds, sometimes thousands) of records.

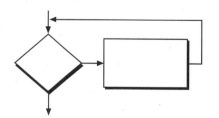

FIGURE 8.1

In addition to this main loop, loops also appear within subroutines. They are used any time a task needs to be done several times and you don't want to write identical or similar instructions over and over.

Consider a very simple program. Suppose you own a factory and have decided to place a sticker or label on every product you manufacture. That sticker has the words "Made for you personally by" and then the name of one of your employees. For starters, you have decided to print 100 personalized stickers for each employee.

You already have an existing personnel file that can be used for input. This file has more information than you'll need for this program. Let's say it has employee name, address, date hired, and salary. The important feature of the file is that it does have each employee's name in one record for each employee. As a programmer, you are probably handed an input file description something like this:

PERSONNEL FILE DESCRIPTION

FILE NAME: EMPLYEES

FIELD DESCRIPTION	*POSITIONS*	*DATA TYPE*	*DECIMALS*
Employee name	*1–30*	*Character*	
Address	*31–50*	*Character*	
Date hired	*51–58*	*Numeric*	*0*
Salary	*59–62*	*Numeric*	*2*

The overall picture of this program could be flowcharted very similarly to all other programs: a housekeeping subroutine (HOUSEKEEP), a main loop (MAIN-LOOP), and a finish routine (FINISH-UP). (See Figure 8.2.)

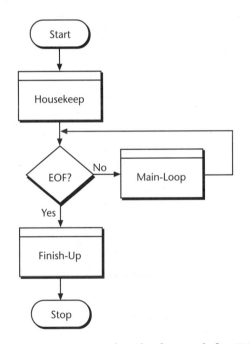

FIGURE 8.2

The HOUSEKEEP routine is very simple. The first task for HOUSEKEEP involves naming the fields on the input record so that they can be referred to within the program. Let's say we've chosen to call the four input fields IN-NAME, IN-ADDRESS, IN-DATE, and IN-SALARY. Starting all the field names in each input record with the same prefix such as IN is a common programming technique to help identify these fields in a large program and differentiate them from work areas and output areas that will have other names.

Using a common prefix on all input field names is definitely not required; it just helps you stay organized. A side benefit is that some language compilers also produce a dictionary of names for you when you compile your program. These dictionaries show at which lines in the program each data name is referenced. If all your input field names start with the same prefix, they will be together alphabetically and perhaps easier to find and work with.

For convenience, we'll also set up a work area in HOUSEKEEP to hold the characters "Made for you personally by". The programmer chooses the name for this area; we'll call ours LABEL-LINE. This LABEL-LINE area will eventually be printed followed by the employee name (IN-NAME).

Another task for housekeeping involves setting up a memory area, which most programmers call a **counter**. This counter is a numeric variable that is used to keep track of how many labels have been printed so far. Each time an employee record is read, this variable is set to zero. Then, every time a label is printed, 1 is added to the variable. Before the next employee label is printed, the variable is checked to see if it has reached 100 yet. When it has, that means 100 labels have been printed, and the job is done for that employee. Since the programmer can choose any name for this counter, we'll choose to call this one LABEL-COUNTER.

Files are always opened at the beginning of a program, and this program is no exception. Therefore, our next major task in HOUSEKEEP is to open the files. The input is an employee file (EMPLYEES according to the EMPLOYEE FILE DESCRIPTION) that is perhaps stored on a disk, so a disk file needs to be opened for input. The output is sent to a printer, so that is another file that needs to be opened.

The last task performed in HOUSEKEEP is to read the first input record. (If you don't know why, go back and look up priming read in Chapters 3 and 6.) The complete HOUSEKEEP is illustrated in Figure 8.3.

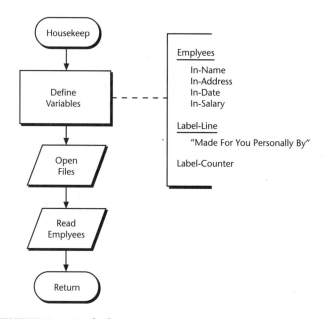

FIGURE 8.3

When HOUSEKEEP is exited, the question EOF? is asked. If, for some reason, the first record is read at the end of HOUSEKEEP and there is no record, the answer to EOF? is yes and the MAIN-LOOP is never entered. Instead, the logic of the program flows directly to FINISH-UP.

Usually, however, there are going to be employee records, and the MAIN-LOOP will be entered. When this happens, the first employee record is sitting in memory waiting to be worked with. During the execution of MAIN-LOOP, 100 labels are printed for one employee. The last thing that happens in MAIN-LOOP is that the next employee record is read. Control of the program then returns to the EOF? question. If that record is not EOF, the MAIN-LOOP is entered again.

The MAIN-LOOP of this label program involves four steps, as shown in Figure 8.4. First, the LABEL-COUNTER is set to 0 (Step 1). Second, LABEL-COUNTER is checked to see if it is 100 (Step 2). If not, a loop to print labels is entered. Two steps take place within the label printing loop. The LABEL-LINE and IN-NAME are printed, and 1 is added to the LABEL-COUNTER (Steps 3 and 4).

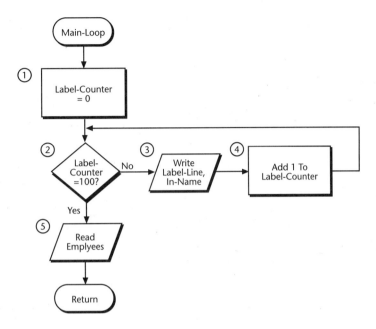

FIGURE 8.4

The label-making loop then returns to the question LABEL-COUNTER = 100? After the first label is printed, the LABEL-COUNTER is only 1. It certainly isn't 100 yet, so the loop is entered for a second time.

After the second printing, LABEL-COUNTER holds a value of 2. Finally, after the 100th label is printed, LABEL-COUNTER has a value of 100, and when the question LABEL-COUNTER = 100? is asked, the answer will finally be yes! The loop is now exited.

In this program, many programmers would call LABEL-COUNTER the loop control variable simply because it controls whether or not the loop will be executed. The number 100 is a constant that would often be called the **limit** or the **sentinel value** for the loop.

Before leaving MAIN-LOOP, after having printed 100 labels for an employee, one final step is performed: the next input record is read from the EMPLYEES file (Step 5). When MAIN-LOOP is over, control returns to the EOF? question in the main line of the logic. If it is not EOF, that is, if another employee record is present, MAIN-LOOP is entered again, LABEL-COUNTER is reset to 0, and 100 new labels are printed with the new employee's name.

At some point, when a new record is read, EOF will be encountered. Then the MAIN-LOOP is not entered again and control passes to the FINISH-UP routine. In this program, that simply means files will be closed. (See Figure 8.5.)

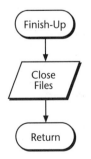

FIGURE 8.5

After 100 labels have been printed for each employee, perhaps it is discovered that some employees are working faster than others and running out of labels sooner. A slightly more sophisticated program than the one that prints 100 labels for each employee might be one that prints a different number of labels for each employee, depending on that employee's last week's production.

Assume that this data exists on an input file called EMPPROD in this format:

EMPLOYEE PRODUCTION FILE DESCRIPTION

FILE NAME: EMPPROD

FIELD	POSITIONS	DATA TYPE	DECIMALS
IN-NAME	1–30	Character	
IN-LAST-PRODUCTION	31–33	Numeric	0

A real-life file would undoubtedly have more fields in each record, but these are all the fields we need to produce the labels. IN-LAST-PRODUCTION is a numeric field that can contain any number from 0 through 999.

The only modification to our original label-making program is in the question that controls the loop. Instead of asking if LABEL-COUNTER = 100, we now ask if LABEL-COUNTER = IN-LAST-PRODUCTION. You see that the limit field can just as easily be a variable as a constant. (See Figure 8.6.)

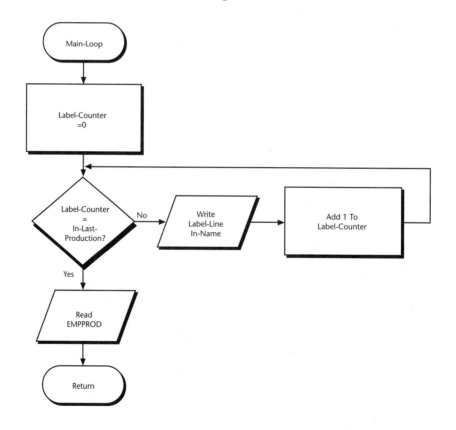

FIGURE 8.6

The two loops discussed in this label-making program—the main loop that controls the program and continues while EOF is not reached and the loop within the MAIN-LOOP that controls the printing of the labels and continues while IN-LAST-PRODUCTION is not reached—look very similar. (See Figure 8.7.) They *should* look similar—they are structured loops.

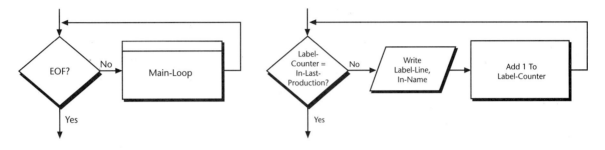

FIGURE 8.7

Every high-level computer language has a **while** statement that could be used to code either of these loops. The statements would be phrased something like this:

> *while not EOF perform MAIN-LOOP*

and

> *while LABEL-COUNTER not = IN-LAST-PRODUCTION*
>   *write LABEL-LINE, IN-NAME*
>   *add 1 to LABEL-COUNTER*

The FOR Statement

Most computer languages also have a **for statement** that could be used to code the label-printing loop. The for statement can be used whenever a loop is to be performed a specific number of times. It would take this form:

> *for LABEL-COUNTER = 0 to IN-LAST-PRODUCTION*
>   *write LABEL-LINE*

If the for statement is available in the language you will be using, you should use it because it has two advantages over the while statement. First, to set LABEL-COUNTER to 0 does not require a separate statement; the for statement does it. Second, the statement to add 1 to LABEL-COUNTER is not needed; the for statement also does that.

Even though these two types of statements are available in most languages, you can see that their logic is the same, and so in flowcharting them, there need be no difference at all.

The Do-Until

Recall from Chapter 3 that there are two kinds of structured loops, as shown in Figure 8.8.

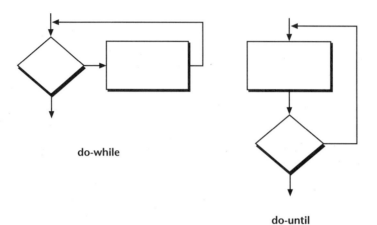

do-while

do-until

FIGURE 8.8

Remember, too, that a do-until is never necessary because a do-until could always be coded as a sequence and then a do-while. For example, let's say you decide that you always want to print at least one label for every employee, even if that employee had zero production last week (maybe because of illness or vacation?). That way, you know that employee's labels weren't just lost—you do have one for every person.

This could be accomplished with a sequence and a do-while (as in Figure 8.9) or with a do-until (as in Figure 8.10).

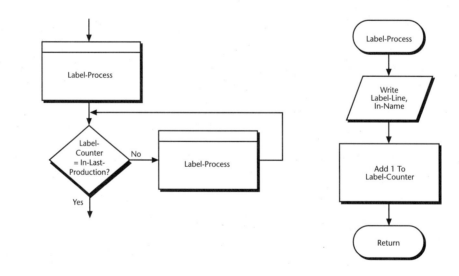

FIGURE 8.9

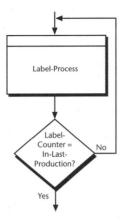

FIGURE 8.10

The biggest difference between a do-while and a do-until is that in the do-while, you might never enter the loop. In the preceding example, if IN-LAST-PRODUCTION is 0, the loop is never entered. With a do-until, the statements in the loop are always done at least once because the test of the sentinel is not done until the end of the loop.

A do-until, then, can be handy. You may use a do-until if the language you're using supports it. If your language doesn't have a do-until (or if you just don't like it), a sequence and a do-while will suffice.

TERMS AND CONCEPTS

review loop
do-while
counter
limit, or sentinel value
for statement
do-until

EXERCISES

 Exercise 1

Design the logic for a program that would print out every number from 1 through 10 along with its square and its cube. Design the print layout chart and create the flow-chart for this program.

 Exercise 2

Assume you have a bank account that compounds interest on a yearly basis. In other words, if you deposited $100 for 2 years at 4% interest, at the end of one year you would have $104. At the end of 2 years, you would have the $104 plus 4% of that, or $108.16.

Draw the logic for a program that would allow you to input a deposit amount, a term, and an interest rate, and print out your running total for each year of the term.

 **Exercise 3**

A school maintains class records in the following format:

CLASS RECORDS FILE DESCRIPTION

FILE NAME: CLASS

FIELD DESCRIPTION	POSITIONS	DATA TYPE	DECIMALS	SAMPLE DATA
Class code	1–6	Character		CIS111
Section no.	7–9	Numeric	0	101
Teacher	10–29	Character		Gable
Enrollment	30–31	Numeric	0	24
Room	32–35	Character		A213

One record is kept for each class section offered in the college. Design the program that would print one name sticker for each student enrolled in each class and one more for the teacher in each class. Each sticker would leave a blank for the student's (or teacher's) name like this:

```
Hello!

My  name  is  _____

Class:  XXXXXX    Section:  999
```

Create the print layout chart, hierarchy chart, and flowchart for this problem.

Control Breaks

Objectives

After studying Chapter 9, you should be able to:

▶ Define a control break report and describe the steps necessary to produce one.

▶ Explain the concept of line counters in multiple-page reports.

▶ Explain the concepts of major, intermediate, and minor control breaks.

A **control break** is a temporary detour in the logic of a program.

Page Breaks

One of the simplest and most common types of control breaks occurs when printed reports have more than one page and new headings are desired at the top of every page. The logic in these programs involves counting the lines printed and, when the counter reaches some predetermined value, pausing to print headings before going on.

Let's say you have a file called EMPLOYEE-FILE. It contains 1000 employees with two character fields that you have decided to call LAST-NAME-IN and FIRST-NAME-IN. You wish to print a list of these employees, 60 detail lines to a page. The main logic of the program should look very familiar. (See Figure 9.1.)

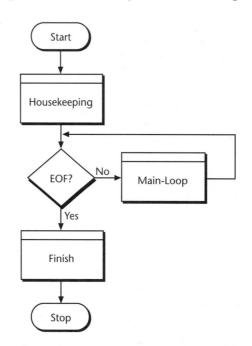

FIGURE 9.1

The usual tasks are performed in HOUSEKEEPING: variables are defined, the files are opened, a HEADINGS routine prints two heading lines at the top of the first page, and a first record is read into memory. (See Figure 9.2.)

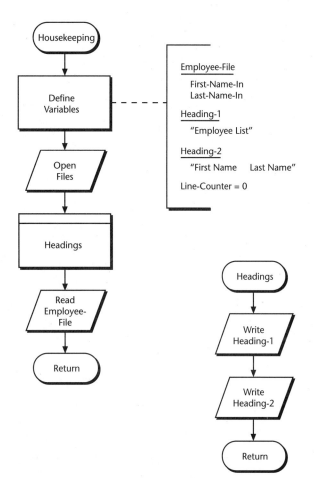

FIGURE 9.2

One of the defined variables is LINE-COUNTER. During execution of the program, every time a line is written, 1 will be added to this counter. When the counter reaches 60, we will pause (or break) to write new headings at the top of a new page before going on.

During the MAIN-LOOP of this program, FIRST-NAME-IN and LAST-NAME-IN are written, 1 is added to LINE-COUNTER, and a new record is read. (See Figure 9.3.)

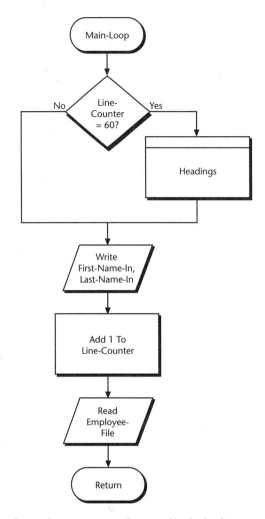

FIGURE 9.3

Before we write any lines, however, we always check the line counter to see if it is 60 yet. After the first record is written, LINE-COUNTER is 1. The second record is then read. If it is not EOF, MAIN-LOOP is entered and the second record is printed. LINE-COUNTER is increased to 2 and the third record is read.

After 60 records have been read and written, LINE-COUNTER holds a value of 60. The sixty-first record is then read, and if it is not EOF, MAIN-LOOP is entered for the 61st time. The question LINE-COUNTER = 60? is asked, and we break or pause to perform the HEADINGS routine. The HEADINGS routine writes the two heading lines at the top of a new page. The logic of the program then returns to MAIN-LOOP, where the 61st record prints out.

After the 61st record prints, 1 is added to LINE-COUNTER. LINE-COUNTER now holds the value 61. This is no good! Every time we reenter MAIN-LOOP, it is checking to see if LINE-COUNTER is 60. If LINE-COUNTER keeps increasing, it will never be 60 again.

In the HEADINGS routine, LINE-COUNTER needs to be set back to 0. That way, when the 61st line prints, LINE-COUNTER will be increased to 1, and it won't hit 60 again until after the 120th line is printed. The new HEADINGS routine is shown in Figure 9.4.

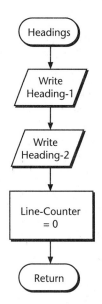

FIGURE 9.4

With one little trick, we can remove the HEADINGS routine from HOUSEKEEPING. If we initialize LINE-COUNTER to 60 when we define the variables at the beginning of the program, on the first pass through MAIN-LOOP we can "fool" the computer into doing the first HEADINGS automatically. HEADINGS can now be taken out of HOUSEKEEPING because when MAIN-LOOP is entered and LINE-COUNTER is determined to be 60 already, HEADINGS will be performed. (See Figure 9.5.)

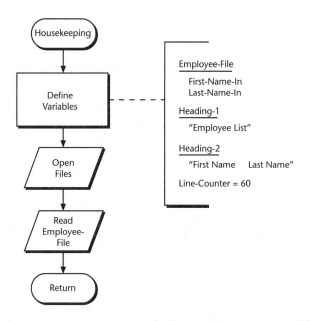

FIGURE 9.5

If you ever need to write a program in which more than one detail line could print per record, it would be a good idea to make the control break question

LINE-COUNTER >= 60?

instead of

LINE-COUNTER = 60?

That way, if LINE-COUNTER happened to be valued at 59 on an occasion when two detail lines were printed, the need for a break would be caught. LINE-COUNTER at a value of 60 or anything higher would force the HEADINGS routine.

Control Breaks with Totals

Suppose you have a bookstore, and one of the files you maintain is a file called BOOK-FILE that has one record for every book that you carry. Each record has fields such as TITLE, AUTHOR, CATEGORY-OF-WORK ("fiction," "reference," "self-help," and so on), PUBLISHER, and PRICE, as shown in this file description:

BOOK FILE DESCRIPTION

FILE NAME: BOOK-FILE

FIELD DESCRIPTION	POSITIONS	DATA TYPE	DECIMALS
Title	1–30		Character
Author	31–46	Character	
Category	47–56	Character	
Publisher	57–72	Character	
Price	73–76	Numeric	2

You could print out a list of all the books that your store carries with the total number of books at the bottom of the list. The main logic of the program would be as shown in Figure 9.6.

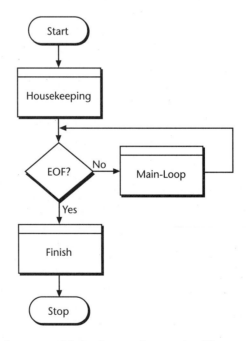

FIGURE 9.6

HOUSEKEEPING then would look as shown in Figure 9.7. A field called GRAND–TOTAL would be set up as a work area and initialized to 0.

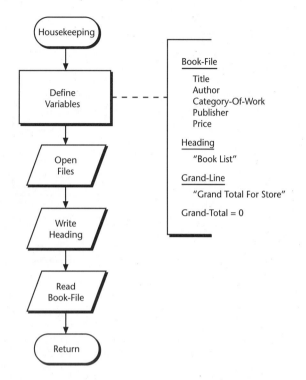

FIGURE 9.7

As illustrated in the flowchart in Figure 9.8, MAIN-LOOP involves three major tasks:

1. Print a book title.
2. Add 1 to the GRAND-TOTAL.
3. Read in the next book record.

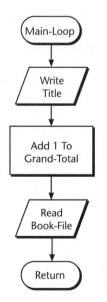

FIGURE 9.8

The FINISH would then take care of the printing of that GRAND-TOTAL. It should be obvious that the printing of the GRAND-TOTAL couldn't take place any earlier in the program because, until the last record has been read, the GRAND-TOTAL isn't complete. (See Figure 9.9.)

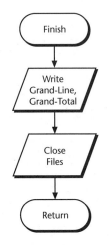

FIGURE 9.9

The logic of the preceding program is pretty straightforward. Suppose, however, that you decided it would be much more useful to have a total for each category of book rather than just one grand total. The desired output would be a list of all fiction books first, followed by a count; then all reference books, followed by a count; and finally all self-help books, followed by a count.

```
BOOK LIST

Abbott's Revenge
Ace in the Hole
.
all these are (fiction titles)
.
Zephyr Madness
      Subtotal for Category        120
ABC's of Home Repair
Amazing Ways With Pasta
.
(all these are reference titles)
.
Your Guide to America's Theme Parks
      Subtotal for Category         87
etc.
      Grand Total for Store        3123
```

A printed report with subtotals is a **control break report**.

In the report just described, during the normal printing of book titles, every once in a while there is a break in the action and control passes to a special set of instructions. In this case, records about books are read into the computer and printed out one by one, but every so often the type of book changes and there is a break or pause while a count is printed for the category of work that just finished printing.

In order for this program to work, one important assumption must be made. The book records must come to the program grouped together by category. In other words, someone must have sorted the input records by CATEGORY-OF-WORK (or *you* must sort them before getting to the report section of your program). If the records aren't arranged by category, they will not print out in groups as we desire.

Some new variables must be defined for this program. A PREVIOUS-CATEGORY variable must be created to which CATEGORY-OF-WORK can be compared. In HOUSEKEEPING, this PREVIOUS-CATEGORY variable can be initialized to hold the value of the first CATEGORY-OF-WORK. A variable to hold the characters "Subtotal for Category" would also be useful. The new HOUSEKEEPING is as shown in Figure 9.10 and the MAIN-LOOP can now look like Figure 9.11.

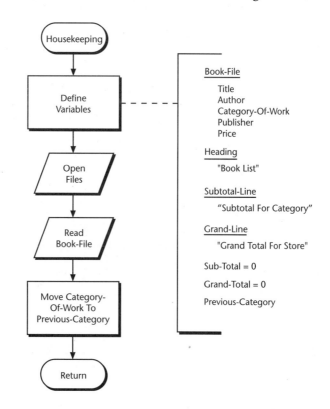

FIGURE 9.10

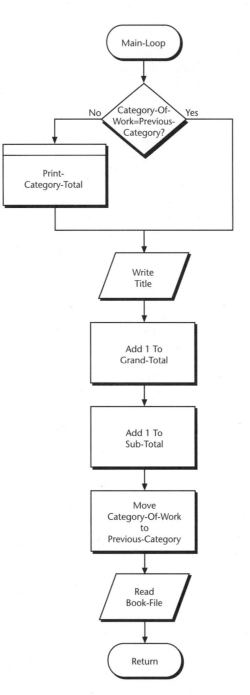

FIGURE 9.11

Every time a record is read and the MAIN-LOOP is entered, the program checks to see if this is a new category of work. It checks by comparing CATEGORY-OF-WORK to the variable called PREVIOUS-CATEGORY. If it is not a new category of work, processing continues as usual with the printing of a line and the adding of 1 to a total.

After the first record is read in HOUSEKEEPING, PREVIOUS-CATEGORY is equal to CATEGORY-OF-WORK, so no subtotal prints the first time MAIN-LOOP is executed. Now, in MAIN-LOOP, instead of just adding 1 to GRAND-TOTAL, let's also add 1 to a SUB-TOTAL for the category. Thus a total is being accumulated for this category as well as for the grand total of all categories.

Before the next record is read, the CATEGORY-OF-WORK is *saved* in the field called PREVIOUS-CATEGORY. This is done by assigning a copy of the contents of the CATEGORY-OF-WORK variable to the PREVIOUS-CATEGORY variable. PREVIOUS-CATEGORY, therefore, always gets its value from the category of book just printed. After the next record is read, if EOF is not encountered, the MAIN-LOOP begins again and a check is made to see if *this* record is a new category of book or if it matches the category of the book just printed. If the new book *does* belong to a new category, a pause in the logic of the program occurs and a subroutine, called PRINT-CATEGORY-TOTAL, is performed that will print out a subtotal for the category of book that just ended.

The PRINT-CATEGORY-TOTAL subroutine not only prints a line with the subtotal for the previous category of books, it should also set the SUB-TOTAL field back to 0 so that when the next category of books starts, it will only have a count of that new category. See Figure 9.12.

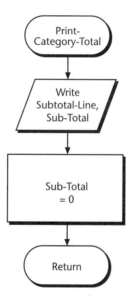

FIGURE 9.12

This program can be improved. Suppose that the first category of books is fiction and that there are 120 fiction titles. In the HOUSEKEEPING routine, PREVIOUS-CATEGORY is set to "fiction." The first time through the MAIN-LOOP, PREVIOUS-CATEGORY equals CATEGORY-OF-BOOK and no break occurs. Then a line is printed, 1 is added to the total, CATEGORY-OF-WORK is moved to PREVIOUS-CATEGORY, and a second record is read.

The CATEGORY-OF-WORK contained in the second record, also "fiction," is moved to PREVIOUS-CATEGORY before the third record is read. The category of the third record, *also* "fiction," is moved to PREVIOUS-CATEGORY before the fourth record is read. The characters in the word "fiction" are moved to a field that already says "fiction"—120 times! That is 119 times too many.

Since the PREVIOUS-CATEGORY field only changes in value when a new category is encountered, why not move the MOVE CATEGORY-OF-WORK TO PREVIOUS-CATEGORY statement to the subroutine that is executed when a new category is encountered, that is, the control break routine PRINT-CATEGORY-TOTAL? This saves the execution of many, many needless instructions.

Here is one last improvement. Currently 1 is added to the SUB-TOTAL, and 1 is added to the GRAND-TOTAL in the MAIN-LOOP. This works fine. In the case of the 120 fiction books, 1 is added to SUB-TOTAL 120 times, and 1 is added to GRAND-TOTAL 120 times. As an alternative, couldn't we just add 1 to SUB-TOTAL and forget about GRAND-TOTAL temporarily? When the control break occurs, the entire SUB-TOTAL with 120 stored in it could be added to GRAND-TOTAL all at once. This means that *one* add instruction would be carried out to add 120 to the GRAND-TOTAL, instead of 120 separate add instructions each adding 1 to the GRAND-TOTAL. Adding the entire SUB-TOTAL to the GRAND-TOTAL in the control break routine is often called **rolling** or **rolling up** the totals to the next level.

The MAIN-LOOP is now as shown in Figure 9.13, and the PRINT-CATEGORY-TOTAL subroutine now looks like Figure 9.14.

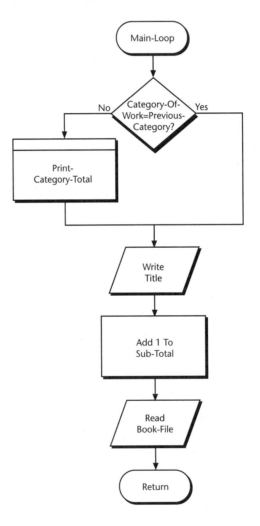

FIGURE 9.13

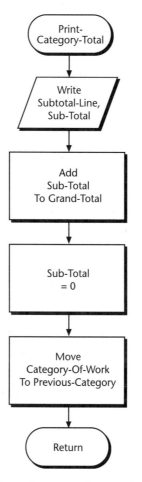

FIGURE 9.14

In general, control break routines always perform at least these four tasks:

1. Print the totals.
2. Roll up the totals.
3. Reinitialize the total fields to 0.
4. Update the control break field.The

FINISH routine for this type of program is more complicated than it may first appear. It seems as though the GRAND-TOTAL should be printed, the files closed, and the routine exited. However, more must be done. Look at the report again:

```
BOOK LIST

Abbott's Revenge
Ace in the Hole
    .
(all these are fiction titles)
    .
Zephyr Madness
        Subtotal for Category     120
ABC's of Home Repair
Amazing Ways With Pasta
    .
(all these are reference titles)
    .
Your Guide to America's
Theme Parks
        Subtotal for Category      87
etc.
        Grand Total for Store    3123
```

At some point, the last book record is read into memory. Let's say it's a self-help book. When this book's title is printed, it is not known that it is the last book. Only when the next read is performed, does the program encounter EOF. Encountering EOF sends the program to the FINISH routine. When the program goes to the FINISH routine, a subtotal for self-help books has not yet been printed and the subtotal for self-help books has not been added into the GRAND-TOTAL. Therefore, before printing a grand total, the FINISH routine must do one chore: perform PRINT-CATEGORY-TOTAL one last time. This final performance of PRINT-CATEGORY-TOTAL then gets the last SUB-TOTAL printed and the last SUB-TOTAL added to GRAND-TOTAL. (See Figure 9.15.)

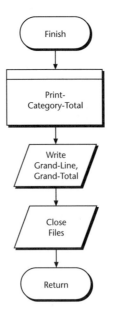

FIGURE 9.15

It is very important to note that this control break program works whether there are three categories of books or 300. Note further that it does not matter what the categories of books are. For example, the program never asks

CATEGORY-OF-WORK = "fiction"?

Instead, the control of the program breaks when the category field changes, and it is in no way dependent on what that change is.

Multiple-Level Control Breaks

Let's say your bookstore from the last example is so successful that you have a chain of them across the country. Every time a sale is made, a record is created with the fields TITLE, PRICE, CITY, and STATE.

You would like a report that prints a summary of books sold in each city and each state. For example,

```
BOOKS SOLD THIS WEEK

Ames              200
Des Moines        814
Iowa City         291

    Total for IA    1305

Chicago          1093
Crystal Lake      564
McHenry           213
Springfield       365

    Total for IL    2235

Springfield       289
Worcester         100

    Total for MA     389

    Grand Total     2929
```

This program would have a **multiple-level control break**. That is, control breaks would occur when CITY changed as well as when STATE changed.

The input file would have to be sorted by CITY *within* STATE. That is, all of one state's records, perhaps IA's, come first, and then all of another state's, maybe IL's. Within any one state like IL, all of one city's records come first and then all of the next city's.

The HOUSEKEEPING routine of this program looks similar to the HOUSE-KEEPING routine in the last control break program. Files are opened and a first record is read. This time, however, there are two fields to save, CITY and STATE. (See Figure 9.16.)

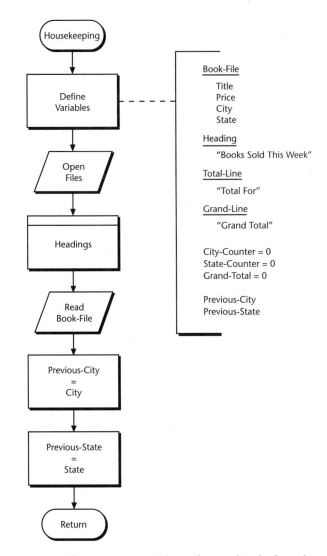

FIGURE 9.16

For a moment, pretend this program prints only one kind of total, a CITY total. The MAIN-LOOP of this program would have only three major tasks:

1. Determine whether or not the current record is from the same city as the previous record.
2. Add 1 to a counter of number of books sold, which could be called CITY-COUNTER.
3. Read in the next record.

When a change occurs in the CITY on the input record, that is, when a new record is read in with a CITY that is different from PREVIOUS-CITY, a break routine called

CITY-BREAK occurs. In CITY-BREAK, the four tasks always performed in a control break routine would happen:

1. Print totals for the PREVIOUS-CITY.
2. Roll up the totals from the CITY-COUNTER to a GRAND-TOTAL.
3. Reinitialize the total field, CITY-COUNTER, to 0.
4. Update the control break field, PREVIOUS-CITY, with the new CITY.

These tasks are reflected in the flowchart in Figure 9.17.

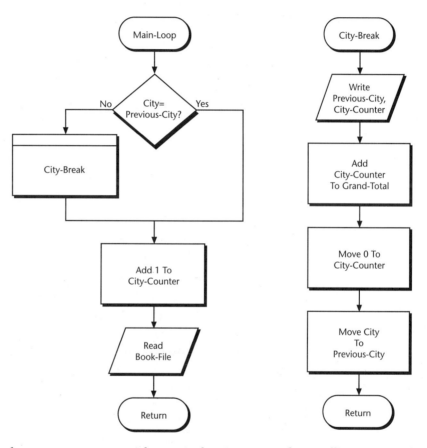

FIGURE 9.17

Since the new program we wish to write has STATE totals as well as CITY totals, we'll have to change the control break routine CITY-BREAK to add the CITY-COUNTER to a STATE-COUNTER instead of a GRAND-TOTAL. So now the CITY-BREAK routine performs these four tasks:

1. Print totals for the PREVIOUS-CITY.
2. Roll up the totals from the CITY-COUNTER to STATE-COUNTER.
3. Reinitialize the total field, CITY-COUNTER, to 0.
4. Update the control break field, PREVIOUS-CITY, with the new CITY.

These tasks are reflected in the flowchart in Figure 9.18.

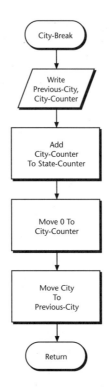

Since state totals are printed in our program, there will also need to be a STATE-BREAK routine in which these four tasks occur:

1. Print totals for the PREVIOUS-STATE.
2. Roll up the totals from the STATE-COUNTER to GRAND-TOTAL.
3. Reinitialize the total field, STATE-COUNTER, to 0.
4. Update the control break field, PREVIOUS-STATE, with the new STATE.

The MAIN-LOOP then would check, not only for any change in CITY, but also for any

change in STATE. When the CITY changes, a CITY total is printed, and when the STATE changes, a STATE total is printed. The question is: Which type of change, CITY or STATE, should MAIN-LOOP check for first?

Recall the desired report:

```
BOOKS SOLD THIS WEEK

Ames          200
Des Moines    814
Iowa City     291

   Total for IA  1305

Chicago       1093
Crystal Lake  564
McHenry       213
Springfield   365

   Total for IL  2235

Springfield   289
Worcester     100

Total for MA      389

   Grand Total   2929
```

Since all the city totals for Iowa print before the state total for Iowa, it might seem logical to check for a change in CITY before checking for a change in STATE. However, the opposite is true!

Consider these possible input records, sorted by CITY within STATE:

TITLE	PRICE	CITY	STATE
A History of Computers	15.99	Ames	IA
The Shining	4.95	Ames	IA
		.	
		.	
		.	
The Gathering	12.00	Ames	IA
Logic for Fun	2.50	Des Moines	IA
Words, Words, Words	9.95	Des Moines	IA
		.	
		.	
		.	
Geography and You	35.00	Iowa City	IA
*The Shining	4.95	Chicago	IL
		.	
		.	
		.	
Logic for Fun	2.50	Springfield	IL
The Senior	10.00	Springfield	IL
**College on a Budget	35.00	Springfield	MA
Interior Decorating	8.25	Springfield	MA
		.	
		.	
		.	

When the first Illinois record (*) is read, Iowa City is stored in the field PREVIOUS-CITY and IA is stored in the field PREVIOUS-STATE. Since CITY and STATE on the new record are both different from the PREVIOUS-CITY and PREVIOUS-STATE fields, both a city and state total will be printed, and it wouldn't really matter which field was checked first.

However, consider the problem when the first record for Springfield, MA, (**) is read. PREVIOUS-STATE is IL, but PREVIOUS-CITY is the same as the current CITY; both are Springfield. If you check for a change in CITY, you won't find one at all, and no city total will get printed even though Springfield, MA, is definitely a different city from Springfield, IL.

The solution is to always check for the **major** break first. If the records were sorted by CITY within STATE, STATE is the major break and CITY would cause a **minor** break. (If our totals were to print by CITY within COUNTY within STATE, we could say we have minor, **intermediate**, and major breaks.) In other words, if there is a change in STATE, there is an implied change in CITY, even if the cities happen to have the same name.

When the major break routine, STATE-BREAK, is performed, the first thing done is the next lower level break; that is, the first step in the STATE-BREAK routine is to perform CITY-BREAK. In STATE-BREAK, the final printing is done for the last CITY in the previous state, and that city's total is added to the state level before the state total is printed.

The MAIN-LOOP then should look like Figure 9.19, and STATE-BREAK looks like Figure 9.20.

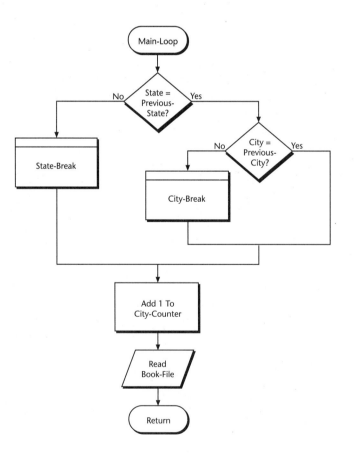

FIGURE 9.19

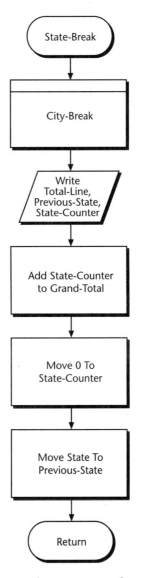

▶ **FIGURE 9.20**

Recall from the previous section that, in general, control break routines always perform at least these four tasks:

1. Print the totals.
2. Roll up the totals.
3. Reinitialize the total fields to 0.
4. Update the control break field.

Now, more accurately, we can say control break routines always perform these five tasks:

1. Perform the next lower level break, if there is a lower level.
2. Print the totals.
3. Roll up the totals.
4. Reinitialize the total fields to 0.
5. Update the control break field.

Finally, the FINISH routine for this control break program must be written.

Perhaps the last 100 records on the BOOK-FILE represent books sold in Worcester, MA. As each one is read into the program, 1 is added to SUBTOTAL. If a new CITY or STATE appeared after the last Worcester, MA, record, then that is when the Worcester subtotal would print because the change in CITY or STATE would cause the control break.

However, there is no new CITY or STATE after Worcester. Records are read in and added to subtotal until EOF is encountered. As soon as EOF is encountered, the MAIN-LOOP sends the program to the FINISH routine. So, when the FINISH routine is entered, neither the Worcester CITY total, nor the MA STATE total has printed.

The FINISH then needs to do both the CITY-BREAK and the STATE-BREAK, but the STATE-BREAK routine performs the CITY-BREAK itself, so all FINISH needs to call is the STATE-BREAK. FINISH then prints the subtotal for the last CITY, the total for the last STATE, and finally, the grand total. (See Figure 9.21.)

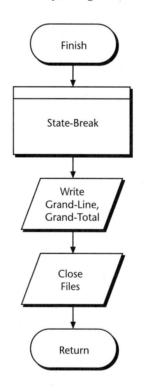

FIGURE 9.21

TERMS AND CONCEPTS

control break
line counter
totals, accumulators
multiple-level control break
major, intermediate, and minor breaks
rolling totals
general tasks performed in control break routines

EXERCISES

 Exercise 1

If a university is organized into colleges (such as Liberal Arts), divisions (such as Languages), and departments (such as French), which would constitute the major, intermediate, and minor control break in a report to print all classes offered by the university?

 Exercise 2

What criteria (or what fields) would you want to use to break down a list of all inventory items in a grocery store?

Exercise 3

A car dealer keeps track of sales in the following format:

AUTO SALES FILE DESCRIPTION

FILE NAME: AUTO

FIELD DESCRIPTION	POSITIONS	DATA TYPE	DECIMALS	EXAMPLE
Salesperson	1–20	Character		Anderson
Make of car	21–30	Character		Ford
Vehicle type	31–40	Character		Van
Sale price	41–45	Numeric	0	18500

By the end of the week, a salesperson may have sold, none, one, or many cars. The input records have been sorted by salesperson.

Create the logic of a program that would print one line for each salesperson with that salesperson's total sales for the week and commission earned, which is 4% of the total sales.

Create the print chart, hierarchy chart, and flowchart.

Exercise 4

A community college maintains student records in the following format:

STUDENT FILE DESCRIPTION

FILE NAME: STUDENTS

FIELD DESCRIPTION	POSITIONS	DATA TYPE	DECIMALS	EXAMPLE
Student name	1–20	Character		June Garcia
City	21–30	Character		Hebron
Hour of first class	31–32	Numeric	0	08
Phone number	33–42	Numeric	0	8154379823

The records have been sorted by hour of the day. Hour of first class is a two-digit number based on a 24-hour clock (that is, a 1 PM first class is recorded as 13).

Create a car pooling report that would list the names and phone numbers of students from the city of Huntley.

Start a new page for each hour of the day so that all students starting at the same hour are listed on the same page. Include the hour that each page represents in the heading. There are never more than 60 students from Huntley starting in a given hour, so no line counter is needed.

It is possible that there is only one student from the city of Huntley starting in a given hour, and even though that student couldn't carpool with anybody, ignore this possibility in your program. Such a student will simply be the only one to print on that page.

Arrays

Objectives

After studying Chapter 10, you should be able to:

- ► Explain the concept of the array or table.
- ► Use a subscript to access an array element.
- ► Explain the difference between a compile-time and an execution-time array.

An **array** is a series of variables in memory, all of which have the same name but are differentiated from each other with special numbers called **subscripts**.

Nested Decisions vs. Arrays

Suppose you had to write a program for a high school that was having a recycling drive. The school is having a competition between the freshman, sophomore, junior, and senior classes to see which class can collect the greatest number of aluminum cans. Each time a student brings in some cans, a record is added to a file in this format:

CAN RECYCLING FILE DESCRIPTION

FILE NAME: STU-RECORDS

FIELD	*POSITIONS*	*DATA TYPE*	*DECIMALS*
STU-CLASS	*1*	*Numeric*	*0*
STU-CANS	*2–4*	*Numeric*	*0*

For example, if a junior brings in 25 cans, one record is created with a 3 (for junior) in the STU-CLASS field and a 25 in the STU-CANS field. If next a freshman brings in 10 cans, a record with 1 and 10 is created. If another junior then brings in 20 cans, the third record will have a 3 and a 20.

Your assignment is to write a program at the end of the recycling competition, after all the records have been collected. The program is to summarize the total of the cans brought in by each class. The report might look like this:

```
CAN COMPETITION REPORT
CLASS      COUNT
1          982
2          765
3          1020
4          1367
```

If all the records were sorted to be in order by STU-CLASS, this could be a control break report. We'd simply read in each record for the first STU-CLASS, accumulating the STU-CANS in a variable. When we encountered a change in class, we'd print out the total for the previous class before continuing.

Let's say, however, that the records have not been sorted. You are handed the file that by this time has over 500 records on it. Could you write the program? Of course you could! The program would have the same overall format of all our previous programs. (See Figure 10.1.)

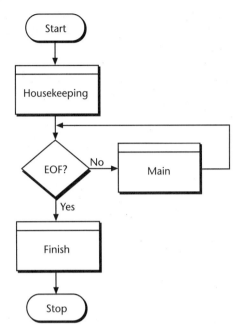

FIGURE 10.1

In HOUSEKEEPING, any needed variables would be declared, the files would be opened, and the first record would be read into memory. The headings *could* be printed in HOUSEKEEPING, or, since no other printing will be done in this program until the FINISH routine, we can choose to wait and print the headings there. (See Figure 10.2.)

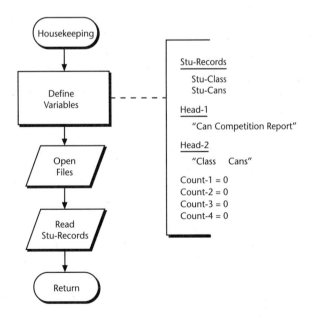

FIGURE 10.2

To keep count of the totals for the four different classes for this program, we are going to need four variables: COUNT-1, COUNT-2, COUNT-3, and COUNT-4. All these counter variables need to be initialized to 0 because we are going to be adding to them.

You can tell by looking at the planned output that two heading lines are needed, so HEAD-1 will be defined as "CAN COMPETITION REPORT" and HEAD-2 as "CLASS   CANS".

Eventually, four lines will be printed, each with a class number and a count of cans for that class. These lines cannot be printed until the FINISH routine, however, because until all input records have been read, we won't have a complete count of each class's cans.

The main logic of our program then is going to involve reading in a record and adding its STU-CANS figure to COUNT-1, COUNT-2, COUNT-3, or COUNT-4, depending on the STU-CLASS. When all records have been accounted for, the four detail lines with the four counts will be printed.

After HOUSEKEEPING, assuming records exist, the MAIN loop of the program will be entered. In this program, no printing is done in MAIN. All that is done in MAIN is that the STU-CANS figure is added to one of the four counters, depending on STU-CLASS. Then the next record is read. If it isn't EOF, control returns to the beginning of this subroutine where another record's STU-CANS is added to an appropriate COUNT. (See Figure 10.3.)

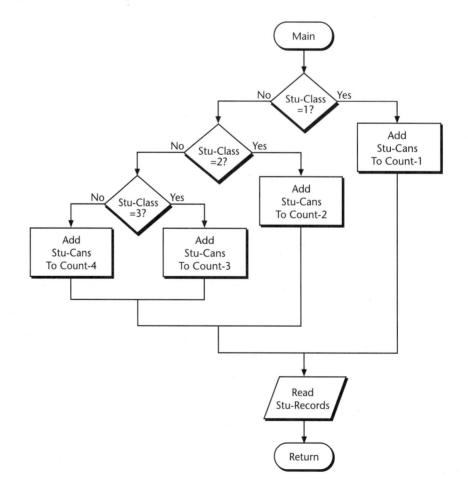

FIGURE 10.3

In FINISH, when all printing is done, the two headings are printed. Then four detail lines are printed. Finally, after the fourth detail line, the files are closed and control returns to the main line logic where the program ends. The flowchart for this FINISH is shown in Figure 10.4.

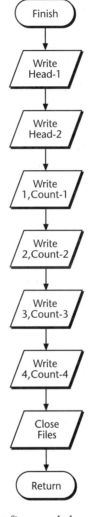

FIGURE 10.4

The preceding program works just fine, and there is absolutely nothing wrong with it logically. But what if this was an elementary school and there were eight classes? Now there would be a lot of decisions in the MAIN loop and a lot of print statements in FINISH. What if instead of a school, it was a corporation with 40 departments?

An **array**, or **table**, is the perfect solution to this programming problem. An array is a number of variables in memory, all of which have the same name. These variables with the same name are differentiated from each other by a number following the variable name. In many languages, this identifying number, called a **subscript**, appears in parentheses () following the variable name. Other languages use brackets [].

A table or array of four variables all called COUNT, then, would have four elements called COUNT(1), COUNT(2), COUNT(3), and COUNT(4). To use a table of four COUNTs in the recycling program, HOUSEKEEPING would be rewritten as shown in Figure 10.5, and MAIN would be as shown in Figure 10.6.

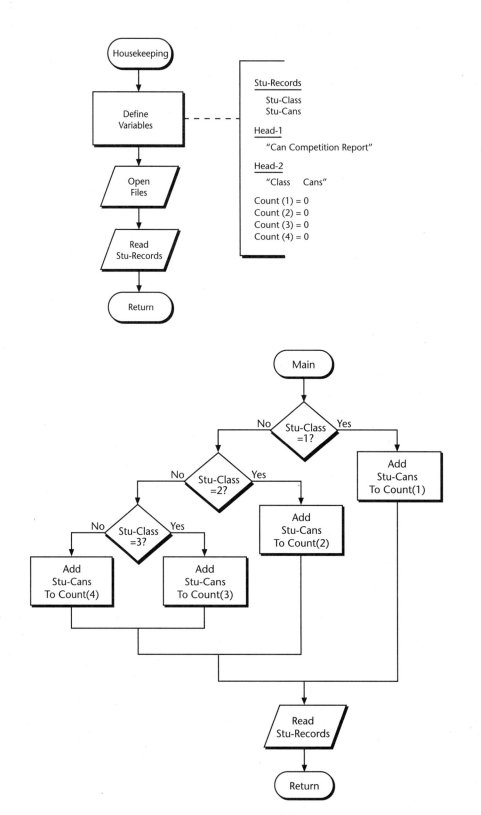

FIGURE 10.5

FIGURE 10.6

When the STU-CLASS is 1, the STU-CANS are added to COUNT(1); when the STU-CLASS is 4, the STU-CANS are added to COUNT(4). Big improvement over the original, huh? Of course it isn't. We have not taken advantage of the benefits of arrays in this program yet.

The true benefit of arrays is the ability to use a variable as a subscript rather than using a constant such as 1 or 4. Notice in the preceding MAIN that in each decision the STU-CLASS and the constant being used as a subscript are always identical. When the STU-CLASS is 1, the subscript used for COUNT is 1; when the STU-CLASS is 2, the subscript used for COUNT is 2; and so on. Therefore, why not just use STU-CLASS as a subscript? The MAIN can be written as shown in Figure 10.7.

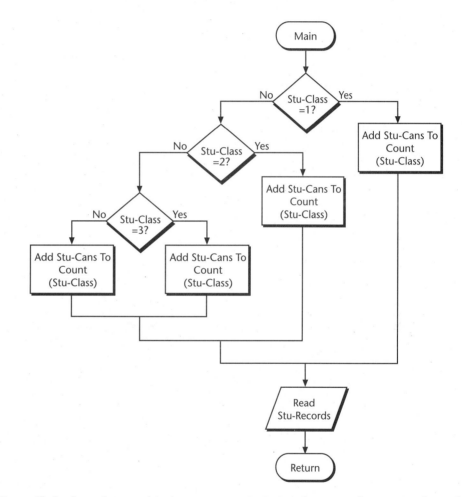

FIGURE 10.7

You still don't notice any big improvement? Notice that now the process box after each decision is exactly the same as every other process box after every other decision. Each box reads ADD STU-CANS TO COUNT(STU-CLASS). If you are always going to take the same action no matter what the answer to a question is, why ask the question? Instead, MAIN can now be written as in Figure 10.8.

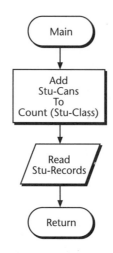

FIGURE 10.8

That's the *whole* thing! When STU-CLASS is 2, STU-CANS is added to COUNT(2); when STU-CLASS is 4, STU-CANS is added to COUNT(4). *Now* do you see the improvement?

The FINISH routine can also be improved upon. Instead of four separate prints, you can use a variable. Since you are in the FINISH routine, all input records have been used and STU-CLASS is not currently holding any needed information. In FINISH, you can set STU-CLASS to 1 and then write STU-CLASS and COUNT(STU-CLASS). If you then add 1 to STU-CLASS, the same set of instructions can be used again and again. (See Figure 10.9.)

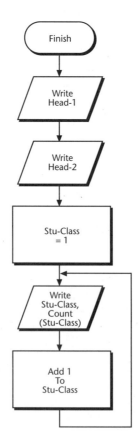

FIGURE 10.9

What's wrong with the flowchart in Figure 10.9? It never ends! We need to add a test. This is really a while situation—while STU-CLASS continues to be 4 or less, keep entering the loop and printing, but as soon as it is 5 or more, stop! Figure 10.10 shows the complete FINISH. Isn't this a big improvement over the original FINISH?

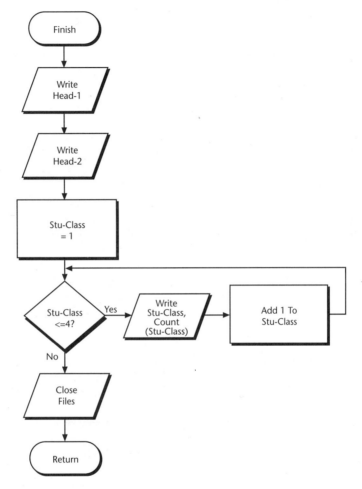

FIGURE 10.10

The STU-CLASS variable was handy to use as a subscript, but any variable could be used as long as it is:

1. A numeric variable with no decimal places, as STU-CLASS is.
2. Set equal to 1, as STU-CLASS is.
3. Incremented by 1 each time the logic passes through the loop, as STU-CLASS is.

The can recycling program *worked* with a long series of decisions, but it was easier to write with arrays. Arrays are never mandatory, but they can often really cut down on your programming time and make a program easier to understand.

Array Initialization

In the can recycling program, the four COUNTS were **initialized** to 0s in the HOUSEKEEPING subroutine. The COUNTs needed to start valued at 0 so that they could be added to during the course of the program. This initialization was depicted simply as:

COUNT(1) = 0
COUNT(2) = 0
COUNT(3) = 0
COUNT(4) = 0

Writing code like this is acceptable only if there are a small number of COUNTs. If the can recycling program were updated to keep track of recycling in a company with 40 departments, 40 fields would have to be initialized. It would be too tedious to write 40 separate initialization statements.

Programming languages do not require the programmer to name each of the 40 COUNTs: COUNT(1), COUNT(2), and so on. Instead, a declaration such as one of these can be made:

Declaration	Language
`DIM COUNT(40)`	BASIC
`int count[40];`	C
`01 COUNT OCCURS 40 TIMES PICTURE 9999.`	COBOL
`ARRAY COUNT [1..40] of INTEGER;`	Pascal

What all these declarations have in common is that they name the fields COUNT and indicate that there will be 40 of them. For flowcharting purposes, a statement such as `ARRAY COUNT (40)` should indicate the same thing to most programmers. Such a declaration statement does not indicate that each of the COUNTs be set to 0. Some programming languages would allow the equivalent of

ARRAY COUNT(40) all set to 0

in which the declaration also initializes.

Other languages would require an **initialization loop** in the HOUSEKEEPING section. To create an initialization loop, a numeric field must be declared to be used as a subscript. Let's declare such a field and call it SUB. If SUB is initialized to 1, then COUNT(SUB) could be set to 0. SUB could be increased by 1, and the next COUNT(SUB) could be set to 0. This would continue until SUB was higher than the number of elements in the array.

A HOUSEKEEPING with an initialization loop might look like Figure 10.11. Of course, if an array is needed in which each element must be set to some unique value, a loop to initialize won't work; but when all array elements should be set to the same value, a loop can quickly accomplish the task.

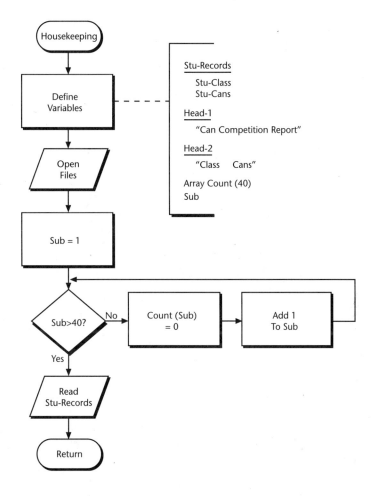

FIGURE 10.11

Run-Time vs. Compile-Time Tables

The table used in the can recycling program could be called a **run-time table**, or **execution-time table**, because the values in the table are created during an actual run, or execution, of the program. In other words, that the freshman class is going to collect 1000 cans isn't known and built in at the beginning of the program. Instead, that value is collected during the execution of the program and not known until the end.

Some tables are not run-time, but rather **compile-time tables**. Recall from Chapter 1 that compiling is the act of translating a high-level language into machine code (1s and 0s). A compile-time table is one whose values are fixed right at the beginning of the program.

For example, let's say you own an apartment building with five floors and you have records for all your tenants with the following information:

TENANT FILE DESCRIPTION

FILE NAME: TENANTS

FIELD	POSITIONS	DATA TYPE	DECIMALS
TENANT-NAME	*1–40*	*Character*	
TENANT-APT	*41–43*	*Numeric*	*0*
TENANT-LEASE-DATE	*44–49*	*Numeric*	*0*

The apartment numbers in your building are all three digits long, and the first number of each apartment number is the same as the floor the apartment is located on. In other words, the tenant in apartment 206 lives on the second floor.

Every month, a rent bill should be printed for each tenant. Your rent charges are based on the floor of the building as follows:

Floor	Rent
1	$350
2	$400
3	$475
4	$600
5	$1000 (the penthouse!)

You want to write a computer program to print out each tenant's name and rent due.

The table that could be used to store the rents is a compile-time table because it is set up once at the beginning of the program and never changes. This is done in the housekeeping routine, which for this program we'll call PREP. There are five RENTs such that RENT(1) = 350, RENT(2) = 400, and so on. The main line logic is shown in Figure 10.12, and PREP is in Figure 10.13.

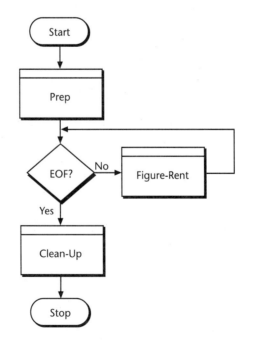

FIGURE 10.12

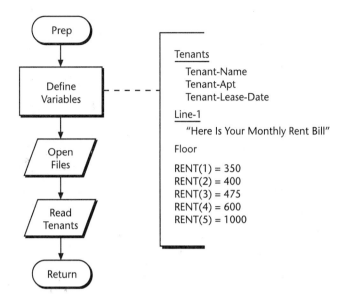

Tenants
   Tenant-Name
   Tenant-Apt
   Tenant-Lease-Date

Line-1
   "Here Is Your Monthly Rent Bill"

Floor

RENT(1) = 350
RENT(2) = 400
RENT(3) = 475
RENT(4) = 600
RENT(5) = 1000

FIGURE 10.13

At the end of PREP, a first record is read into memory. When FIGURE-RENT (the main loop) is entered, LINE-1 (which contains "Here Is Your Monthly Rent Bill") is printed. The next line should print out the TENANT-NAME from the input record and the rent due.

Different languages provide different techniques for determining the floor on which the tenant lives, but one possibility would be to divide the tenant's apartment number by 100 and ignore the fractional remainder. In other words, if apartment 419 is divided by 100, the result is 4.19. If the fractional (decimal) portion is dropped, 4 remains, which corresponds to the floor where apartment 409 is. Just how this fractional part of the quotient is dropped is done slightly differently in different languages, but all languages have the capability. Therefore, we'll take the TENANT-APT and divide by 100, producing a whole-number field that we'll name FLOOR.

One way to find the rent would be to make a series of selections like "If FLOOR = 1 then write TENANT-NAME, RENT (1)" and "If FLOOR = 2 write TENANT-NAME, RENT (2)", and so on. But this does not take advantage of the capabilities of arrays. (See Figure 10.14.)

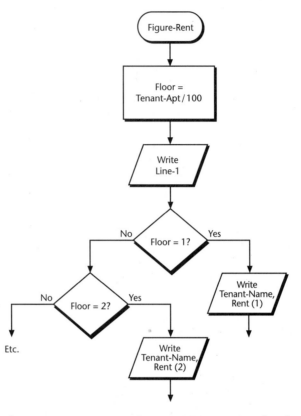

FIGURE 10.14

The much easier solution is to create a FIGURE-RENT routine that looks like Figure 10.15. Since the rent is based on the first digit of the apartment number, just use the calculated FLOOR as a subscript. As each tenant's record is read in, his or her correct rent is printed out.

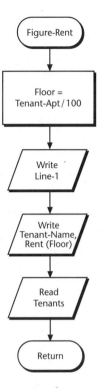

FIGURE 10.15

The CLEAN-UP to this program is very simple—just close the files. (See Figure 10.16.)

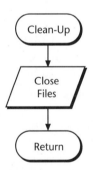

FIGURE 10.16

Arrays or tables then can really lighten the load!

Searching an Array for an Exact Match

Perhaps you didn't notice, but in both the rent program and the recycling program, the fields that the tables depended on were conveniently small whole numbers. The floors of the building were 1 through 5 and the classes in the school were 1 through 4. Unfortunately real life doesn't always happen in small whole numbers.

Consider this situation. You have a mail order business. An order comes in with a customer name, address, item number ordered, and quantity ordered:

CUSTOMER FILE DESCRIPTION

FILE NAME: CUST-REC

FIELD	POSITIONS	DATA TYPE	DECIMALS
CUST-NAME	1–20	Character	
CUST-ADD	21–40	Character	
CUST-ITEM-NO	41–43	Numeric	0
CUST-QUANTITY	44–45	Numeric	0

Your item numbers are three-digit numbers, but perhaps they are not consecutive 001 through 999. Instead, over the years, items have been deleted and new items have been added, so that, for example, there may no longer be an 005 or a 129. Sometimes there may be a hundred number gap or more between items.

Let's say that this season you are down to these items:

ITEM-NO	ITEM-PRICE
006	0.59
008	0.99
107	4.50
405	15.99
457	17.50
688	39.00

You want to write a program to read in a customer's order, find the price of the ordered item, multiply that price by quantity ordered, and print out a bill.

You could write a program in which you would read in a customer order record and then use CUST-ITEM-NO as a subscript to pull a price from an array. You would need an array with at least 688 elements. If a customer ordered item 405, the price would then be found at TABLE-PRICE(405), or the 405th element of the array. Such an array would have a lot of wasted space—682 empty slots to be exact—and that would use up a lot of memory for nothing. Instead, what this program needs is two arrays.

Consider the main line logic and READY routine in Figure 10.17. Two arrays are set up in READY. The one called TABLE-OF-NOS has six elements, all valid item numbers; the other, TABLE-OF-PRICES has six elements, all prices. Each price in this array is conveniently in the same position as the corresponding item number in the other array.

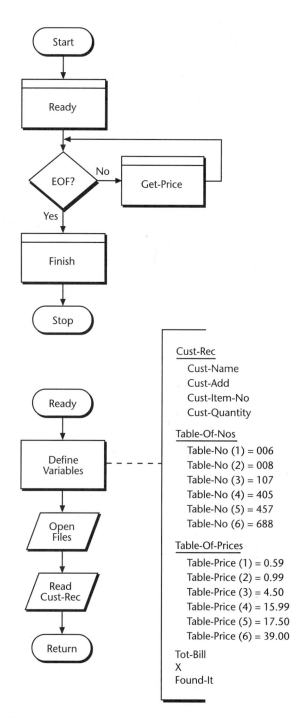

FIGURE 10.17

Now, the GET-PRICE routine can be written as shown in Figure 10.18. The general procedure is to read each item number, look through the TABLE-OF-NOS one at a time, and when a match for the CUST-ITEM-NO on the input record is found, pull the corresponding price out of the TABLE-OF-PRICES.

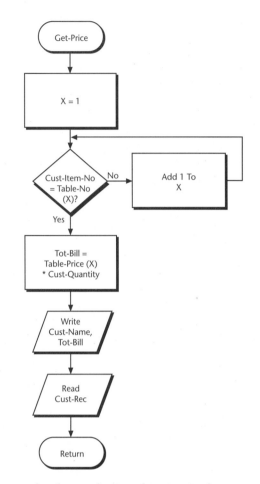

FIGURE 10.18

A variable can be created to be used as a subscript. Let's say we decide to call it X. X can be set equal to 1. Then, if CUST-ITEM-NO is the same as TABLE-NO (X), the corresponding price from the other table, TABLE-PRICE (X), can be multiplied by the quantity ordered and the bill can be written.

If CUST-ITEM-NO is *not* the same as TABLE-NO (X), then 1 can be added to X. Since X now holds a value of 2, TABLE-NO (2) is compared to the order number. X keeps increasing, and eventually, a match between CUST-ITEM-NO and TABLE-NO (X) is found.

Once we know the position of CUST-ITEM-NO in TABLE-OF-NOS, we know that the price of that item is in the same position in the other table, TABLE-OF-PRICES. When TABLE-NO (X) is the correct item, TABLE-PRICE (X) must be the correct price.

Suppose that someone ordered item 457 and walk through the flowchart yourself to see if you come up with the correct price.

The preceding program is not perfect. We have made one dangerous assumption: that every customer is going to order a valid item number. If a customer is looking at an old catalog and orders item 007, our program is going to go into an infinite loop. Try it!

An improvement would be a check to see if we've gone through the whole table without finding a matching item number. We'll need to make use of a **flag**.

In READY, set up a flag field called FOUND-IT (or any other name you choose). When we enter the GET-PRICE routine, set FOUND-IT equal to "NO". Then after setting X to 1, check to see if X is greater than 6 yet. If it is, you shouldn't look through the table any more; you've gone through all 6 legitimate items and you've reached the end.

In some languages, your program would stop automatically if X became greater than 6; these languages would keep track of how big your array was supposed to be and prevent you from looking past it. In other languages, X could keep getting bigger and bigger, and you could spend a lot of time looking through all of computer memory for a price. In either case, you *should* stop looking when X becomes greater than 6, and it is up to the programmer to provide for this. (See Figure 10.19.)

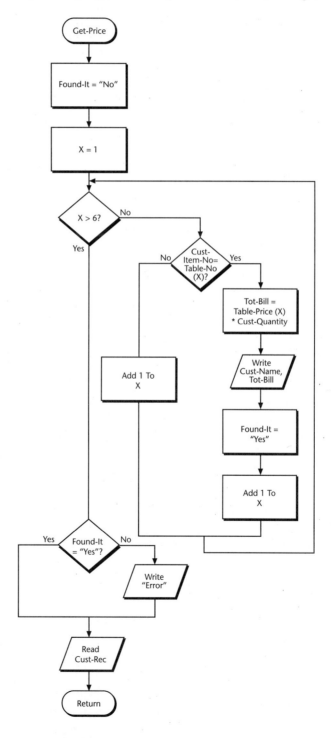

FIGURE 10.19

A loop is created that is entered only if X is 6 or less. Inside the loop, the logic is the same as before. If CUST-ITEM-NO is equal to TABLE-NO (X), you know the item number's position, so you know the price's position and you can print the correct price. Now, if you find the item number, you also set FOUND-IT to "YES" and add 1 to X.

After you look at the sixth item number, X is increased to 7. X is then greater than 6, so you'll leave the loop. If, at this point FOUND-IT doesn't have a "YES" in it, it means you never found a match for the ordered item number; you never took the yes path leading from CUST-ITEM-NO = TABLE-NO(X). If FOUND-IT does not have "YES" stored in it, you should print out an error message.

Checking X for a value greater than the number of table elements and using the FOUND-IT flag have really helped in two ways—as a means for stopping the loop from executing infinitely and as a cue to print an error message if an item number can't be found.

This program is still a little inefficient. The problem lies in the fact that if lots of customers order item 006 or item 008, even after their price has been found on the first or second pass through the loop, the program still looks through the rest of the item numbers before X hits 7 and the searching stops. Once the item has been found and FOUND-IT set to "YES", why not force X to 7 immediately? Then, when the program loops back to check whether or not X is greater than 6 yet, the loop will be exited and the program won't bother checking any of the higher item numbers.

Here, then, is the final version of the GET-PRICE loop. The table is searched. If an item number is not found in a given location, the subscript is increased and the next location is checked. As soon as an item number is located in the table, a line is printed, a flag is turned on, and the subscript is forced to a high number so the program will not check the item number table any further. (See Figure 10.20.)

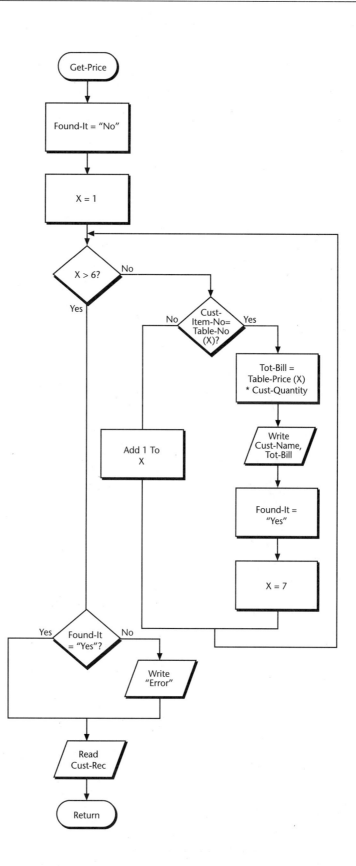

FIGURE 10.20

Searching an Array for a Range Match

Item numbers need to match exactly in order to determine the price of an item. Sometimes, however, programmers want to work with ranges of values in arrays.

Recall the customer file description from the last section:

CUSTOMER FILE DESCRIPTION

FILE NAME: CUST-REC

FIELD	POSITIONS	DATA TYPE	DECIMALS
CUST-NAME	1–20	Character	
CUST-ADD	21–40	Character	
CUST-ITEM-NO	41–43	Numeric	0
CUST-QUANTITY	44–45	Numeric	0

Suppose the company decides to offer quantity discounts on the following basis:

Size of Order	Discount
1–9 items	None
10–24 items	10%
25–48 items	15%
49 or more items	25%

You want to be able to read in a record and, based on the value in the CUST-QUANTITY field, determine a discount percentage.

One approach would be to set up an array with as many elements as any customer might ever order, and store the appropriate discount for each possible number:

DISCOUNT(1)=0%
DISCOUNT(2)=0%

.
.
.

DISCOUNT(9)=0%
DISCOUNT(10)=10%

.
.
.

DISCOUNT(48)=15%
DISCOUNT(49)=25%
DISCOUNT(50)=25%

.
.
.

This approach has two problems:

1. It requires a very large array that uses a lot of memory.
2. Where do you stop anyhow? Are 75 items high enough? 100? 1000? No matter how many elements you place in the array, there's a chance that some day a customer will order more.

A better approach would be to create just four discount array elements, one for each of the possible discount rates:

DISCOUNT(1) = 0%
DISCOUNT(2) = 10%
DISCOUNT(3) = 15%
DISCOUNT(4) = 25%

What we would then like to do is create another array to search through to find the appropriate discount level. At first, many students think they would like to create an array element such as

RANGE(1) = 1 through 9

and test to see if CUST-QUANTITY matches this value. The problem is that RANGE(1) is simply a variable. It can hold a 1 or it can hold a 9, but it can't hold a 1 *through* 9; there is no such numeric value. Your boss can pay you $5.00 per hour or she can pay you $100.00 per hour, but it is impossible to pay you $5.00 through $100.00 per hour. There is no such numeric value.

So, let's simply place the lowest value of each range in an array of ranges:

RANGE(1) = 1
RANGE(2) = 10
RANGE(3) = 24
RANGE(4) = 49

Now, the process is to compare each CUST-QUANTITY with the *last* range limit (RANGE(4)). If the CUST-QUANTITY is:

- At least that value, the customer gets the highest discount rate (DISCOUNT(4)).
- Not at least RANGE(4), see if it is at least RANGE(3). If so, the discount is DISCOUNT(3).
- Not at least RANGE(3) and is at least RANGE(2), the discount is DISCOUNT(2).
- Not at least RANGE(2), there *is no* discount, which is DISCOUNT(1).

Assuming you have created a variable called DISC-RATE to hold the discount percentage so that math may be performed with it later, the logic to determine the rate is as depicted in Figure 10.21.

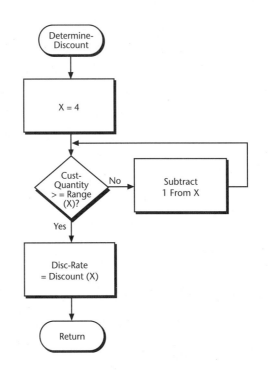

FIGURE 10.21

Multidimensional Arrays

All the arrays discussed so far in this chapter are called **single-dimensional arrays** because they represent data in a single column. The rent table had five elements that could be represented in one column like this:

RENT(1) =   350
RENT(2) =   400
RENT(3) =   475
RENT(4) =   600
RENT(5) = 1000

The values of the RENTs depended only on a single variable—the floor of the building. Sometimes, however, the values in an array depend on more than one variable.

Let's assume that the floor is not the only factor determining rent in your building, but that another variable, NUMBER-OF-BDRMS, also needs to be taken into account. The rent schedule might be:

Floor	1 Bdrm	2 Bdrm	3 Bdrm
1	350	390	435
2	400	440	480
3	475	530	575
4	600	650	700
5	1000	1075	1150

Each element of a **two-dimensional array** needs two subscripts to reference it—one subscript to determine the row, and a second to determine the column. Thus the RENT values for a two-dimensional array based on the preceding values would be:

RENT(1,1) = 350
RENT(1,2) = 390
RENT(1,3) = 435
RENT(2,1) = 400
RENT(2,2) = 440
RENT(2,3) = 480

.
.
.

RENT(5,3) = 1150

Now, if two variables, FLOOR and NUMBER-OF-BDRMS, were read from the input file, the appropriate rent could be printed out with the statement:

WRITE RENT(FLOOR,NUMBER-OF-BDRMS)

Two-dimensional arrays are never actually *required*. The same information could be stored in three separate single-dimensional arrays of five elements each as follows:

ARRAY BR-ONE	ARRAY BR-TWO	ARRAY BR-THREE
BR-ONE(1) = 350	BR-TWO(1) = 390	BR-THREE(1) = 435
BR-ONE(2) = 400	BR-TWO(2) = 440	BR-THREE(2) = 480
BR-ONE(3) = 475	BR-TWO(3) = 530	BR-THREE(3) = 575
BR-ONE(4) = 600	BR-TWO(4) = 650	BR-THREE(4) = 700
BR-ONE(5) = 1000	BR-TWO(5) = 1075	BR-THREE(5) = 1150

and rent could be determined as shown in Figure 10.22.

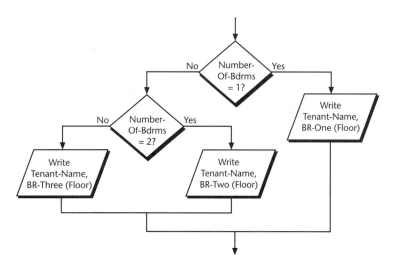

FIGURE 10.22

Of course, don't forget that arrays are never *required*. Fifteen separate decisions could always be made to determine the rent. Single-dimensional arrays make the rent-determining process easier, and two-dimensional arrays help even more.

Some languages allow **three-dimensional arrays**. For example, rent might not only be determined by the two factors, FLOOR and NUMBER-OF-BDRMS. There might also be twelve different buildings. The third dimension of a three-dimensional array to hold all these different rents would be a variable like BUILDING-NUMBER.

Some languages allow even more dimensions. It's usually hard for humans to mentally keep track of more than three dimensions, but if rent was determined by floor number, number of bedrooms, building number, city number, and state number, you might want to try to use a **five-dimensional array**.

TERMS AND CONCEPTS

array, table
subscript (index)
initialization loop
run-time table
compile-time table
execution time table
flag
single-dimensional array
two-dimensional array
multidimensional array

EXERCISES

Exercise 1

The city of Cary has taken a special census, and one record for each citizen has been collected.

CENSUS FILE DESCRIPTION

FILE NAME: CENSUS

FIELD DESCRIPTION	POSITIONS	DATA TYPE	DECIMALS
Age	1–3	Numeric	0
Gender	4	Character	
Marital Status	5	Character	
Voting District	6–7	Numeric	0

The voting district field contains integers from 01 through 22.

Design the report for, draw the hierarchy chart for, and draw the logic of the program that would produce a count of the number of citizens in each of the 22 districts.

Exercise 2

Using the same CENSUS file from Exercise 1, create a report that would produce a count of citizens in each of the following age categories:

0–12
13–20
21–35
36–65
66 and over

Exercise 3

A fast food restaurant sells the following products:

Product	Price
Cheeseburger	2.49
Pepsi	1.00
Chips	.59

Write a program that would accept an item as input, and print either the correct price, or the message "Sorry, we do not carry that" as output.

 Exercise 4

Modify Exercise 1 to accept any number of inputs (one at a time) until EOF and keep a running total of the bill. Before the final total is printed, add in sales tax, which is 6% of the bill.

 Exercise 5

A company desires a breakdown of payroll by department. Input records are as follows:

PAYROLL FILE DESCRIPTION

FILE NAME: PAY

FIELD DESCRIPTION	POSITIONS	DATA TYPE	DECIMALS	EXAMPLE
Employee name	*1–20*	*Character*		*Ann Norris*
Department	*21*	*Numeric*	*0*	*3*
Hourly salary	*22–26*	*Numeric*	*2*	*12.50*

Input records come in alphabetical order by employee, *not* in department number order.

The output is a list of the seven departments in the company (numbered 1 through 7) and the total payroll for each department.

Create the print layout chart, hierarchy chart, and flowchart for this program.

 Exercise 6

Create the same report as in Exercise 5, but have the output list department names as well as numbers. The names are:

Department Number	Department Name
1	Personnel
2	Marketing
3	Manufacturing
4	Computer Services
5	Sales
6	Accounting
7	Shipping

Exercise 7

Create the same report as in Exercise 6, but before the department totals are printed at the end of the report, list each employee, his or her department, his or her hourly wage, his or her gross pay based on a 40-hour week, and his or her withholding tax.

Withholding taxes are based on the following percentages:

Weekly Salary	Withholding Percent
0.00–200.00	10%
200.01–350.00	14%
350.01–500.00	18%
500.01–up	22%

Create the print layout chart, hierarchy chart, and flowchart for this program.

CHAPTER

11

Sorting, Indexing, and Linked Lists

Objectives

After studying Chapter 11, you should be able to:

- List reasons for sorting records.
- Explain the differences among a bubble sort, an insertion sort, and a selection sort.
- Describe the disadvantages of sorting and explain when it is an inappropriate procedure.
- Explain the concept of indexing.
- Explain the concept of a linked list.

Often data is arranged in some order other than the order desired for processing or viewing. When this is the case, the data needs to be **sorted**. Here are some examples:

- A college student's record contains data on every course in which she has ever been enrolled. This data is stored in chronological order by semester, but the registrar wants to view the data by academic department to determine if graduation requirements have been met.
- A company stores bills it has sent its customers in customer number order, but at the end of a billing period, it wants to extract those records that are 90 or more days overdue and display them in order of the amount owed so the customers maintaining the biggest debt can be contacted first.
- Certain statistics, like **median** (middle value of a list, *not* the same as the average, or **mean**) require an ordered list.

Keep in mind that sorting is usually reserved for a relatively small number of data items. If thousands of customer records are stored and they frequently need to be accessed in order based on different fields (alphabetical order by customer name one day, zip code order the next), the records would probably not be sorted at all, but would be **indexed**, or **linked**. Indexing and linking are discussed at the end of this chapter.

Bubble Sort

Many sorting techniques have been developed. We'll deal first with one technique commonly called the **bubble sort**. In a bubble sort, items in a list are compared in pairs, and when an item is out of order, it trades places with the item below it. After each adjacent pair of items in a list has been compared once, the largest item in the list has "bubbled" to the bottom. After many passes through the list, the smallest items rise to the top, like bubbles.

Let's assume that five student test scores have been stored in a file, and we wish to sort them from lowest to highest for printing. To begin, we'll define three subroutines: HOUSEKEEPING, SORT-SCORES, and FINISH. (See Figure 11.1.)

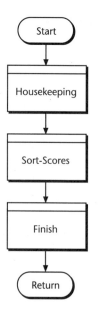

FIGURE 11.1

The HOUSEKEEPING routine of this program defines a variable name for each individual score on the input file and sets up an array of five elements in which to store the five scores. The entire file is then read into memory and one score is stored in each element of the array. (See Figure 11.2.)

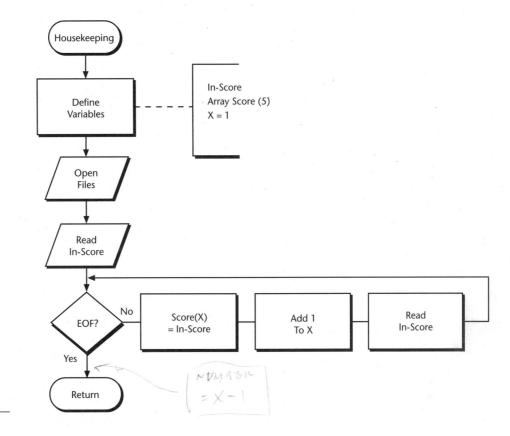

FIGURE 11.2

When the **SORT-SCORES** routine is entered, five scores have been placed in the array. Perhaps they are:

SCORE(1) = 90
SCORE(2) = 85
SCORE(3) = 65
SCORE(4) = 95
SCORE(5) = 75

The general sorting procedure is going to involve comparing the first two scores, and if they are out of order, reversing them.

How do you reverse two scores? SCORE(1) is 90 and SCORE(2) is 85. If we move SCORE(1) to SCORE(2), both SCORE(1) and SCORE(2) hold 90 and the value 85 is lost. Similarly, if we move SCORE(2) to SCORE(1), both variables will hold 85 and the 90 will be lost.

The solution lies in the creation of a TEMP variable to hold one of the scores. The switch can then be accomplished as shown in Figure 11.3. The 85 is moved to the temporary holding variable, TEMP. Then the 90 is moved to SCORE(2). The 85 in TEMP is then moved to SCORE(1).

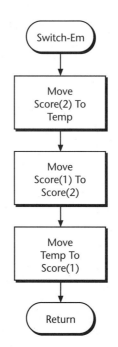

FIGURE 11.3

This SWITCH-EM routine is limited in use because it only switches elements 1 and 2 of the array. The more universal SWITCH-EM shown in Figure 11.4 switches *any* two adjacent elements in an array where X in the flowchart is the position of the first of the two elements.

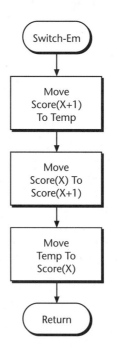

FIGURE 11.4

SWITCH-EM needs to be performed whenever any Xth element of the SCORE array has a greater value than the X+1th element of the array. If the Xth element is not greater than the one following it, the switch should not take place. (See Figure 11.5.)

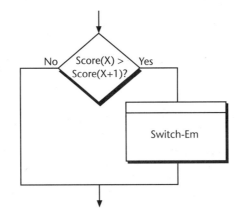

FIGURE 11.5

The decision SCORE(X) > SCORE(X+1)? needs to be performed four times, when X is 1, 2, 3, and 4. It should not be performed when X is 5 because then SCORE(5) would be compared to SCORE(5+1) and there is no valid SCORE(6) in the array. Therefore, the loop evolves to the one shown in Figure 11.6.

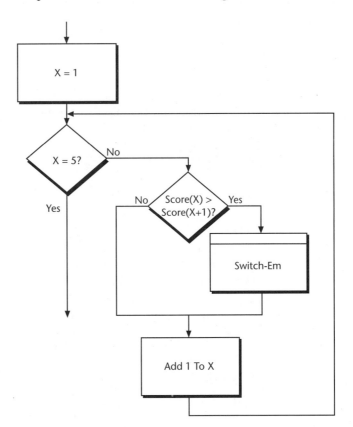

FIGURE 11.6

If we are working with these original scores:

SCORE(1) = 90
SCORE(2) = 85
SCORE(3) = 65
SCORE(4) = 95
SCORE(5) = 75

then the logic proceeds like this:

1. X is set to 1.
2. X is not 5 so SCORE(X), 90, is compared with SCORE(X+1), 85.
3. The two SCOREs are out of order, so they are switched.
4. The list is now:

SCORE(1) = 85
SCORE(2) = 90
SCORE(3) = 65
SCORE(4) = 95
SCORE(5) = 75

5. 1 is added to X, so X is 2.
6. SCORE(X) is compared to SCORE(X+1).
7. They are out of order, so they are switched, resulting in:

SCORE(1) = 85
SCORE(2) = 65
SCORE(3) = 90
SCORE(4) = 95
SCORE(5) = 75

8. 1 is added to X, so X is now 3.
9. SCORE(X) is compared to SCORE(X+1) and they are in order. No switch is made.
10. 1 is added to X, making it 4.
11. SCORE(4) is larger than SCORE(5), so they are switched, giving:

SCORE(1) = 85
SCORE(2) = 65
SCORE(3) = 90
SCORE(4) = 75
SCORE(5) = 95

12. 1 is added to X. X is 5, and the loop ends. Every element in the list has been compared with the one adjacent to it. The highest score, a 95, has "sunk" to the bottom of the list.

The scores, however, are still not in order. They are in slightly better order than they were to begin with, but they are still out of order. The entire procedure needs to be repeated so that 85 and 65 can switch places and 90 and 75 can switch places.

As a matter of fact, if the scores had started out in the worst possible order: 95, 90, 85, 75, 65, the process would have to take place four times. So, the worst-case routine looks Figure 11.7. In other words, with five elements in an array, it takes four comparisons to get through the array once, and it takes four sets of those comparisons to get the entire array in sorted order.

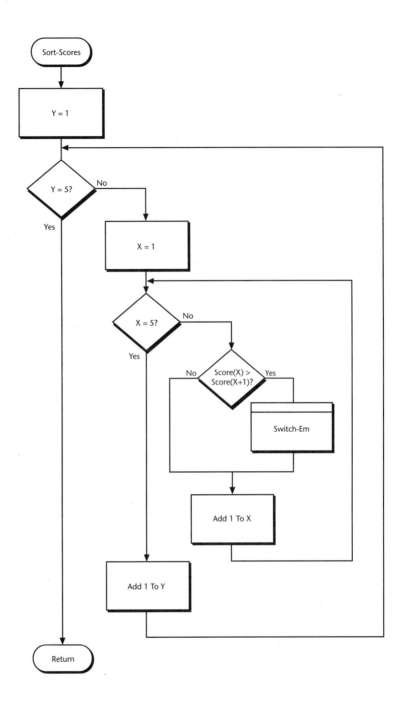

FIGURE 11.7

The more general rule is that whatever the number of elements in the array, it takes one less comparison and one less set of such comparisons to sort the array. If the number of elements in the array can be stored in a variable named NUMBER-ELS, the general logic is as shown in Figure 11.8.

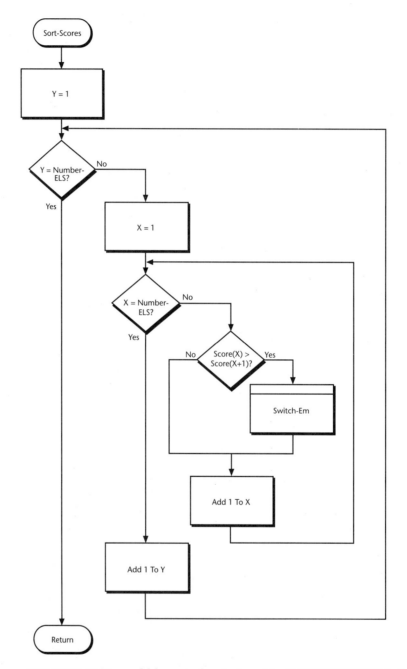

FIGURE 11.8

Of course, NUMBER-ELS would have to be declared in HOUSEKEEPING. It could be set to 5 there because we know there are five elements in the array to be sorted. A more flexible approach would be to add one additional statement at the end of the

HOUSEKEEPING subroutine. When the IN-SCOREs are read during HOUSE-KEEPING, X is increased by 1 for each IN-SCORE read. After EOF is encountered, NUMBER-ELS should simply be set equal to X – 1. Then, if there are not enough IN-SCOREs to fill the array, we can pass through the array making only one fewer than NUMBER-ELS pair comparisons instead of always making four pair comparisons.

Now the FINISH routine of the program could easily list the SCOREs in order, as shown in Figure 11.9

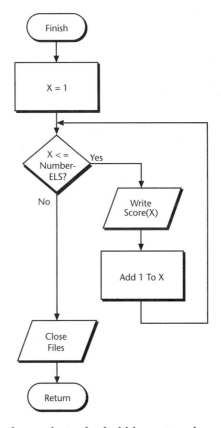

FIGURE 11.9

Two improvements can be made to the bubble sort we have created. One improvement involves the fact that even though the largest value is guaranteed to be at the bottom of the list after the first set of comparisons is done, we continue to compare the bottom two elements with each other on every subsequent set of comparisons. (That's because we always perform the comparisons NUMBER-ELS – 1 times.) Similarly, the second largest element is guaranteed to be in the second-to-last position after the second pass through the list, and so on.

We could actually afford to stop our pair comparisons one element sooner on each pass through the array. This can be accomplished by setting a new variable, PAIRS-TO-COMPARE, to the value of NUMBER-ELS – 1. On the first pass through the list, every pair of elements is compared, so PAIRS-TO-COMPARE *should* equal NUMBER-ELS – 1. But, for each subsequent pass, PAIRS-TO-COMPARE should be reduced by 1 because, after the first pass, there's no need to check the bottom element any more. (See Figure 11.10.)

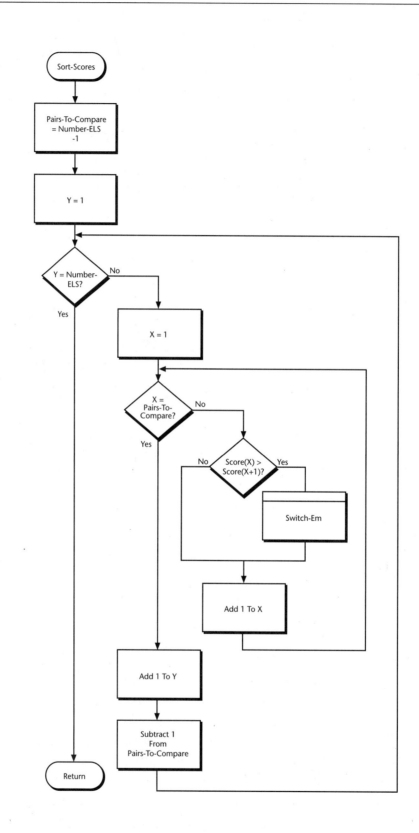

 FIGURE 11.10

A second improvement that could be made to the bubble sort concerns the number of passes through the array that are made. What if the scores were originally read in as:

SCORE(1) = 65
SCORE(2) = 75
SCORE(3) = 85
SCORE(4) = 90
SCORE(5) = 95

Our bubble sort program would pass through the array four times making four sets of pair comparisons. It would always find SCORE(X) *not* greater than SCORE(X+1), so no switches would ever be made. The scores would end up in the proper order, but they *were* in the proper order in the first place! A lot of time has been wasted.

A possible remedy is to add a flag. We'll call it SWITCH-OCCURRED and we'll set it to "NO" at the start of each pass through the list. We'll change its value to "YES" each time the SWITCH-EM subroutine is performed (that is, each time a switch is necessary).

If we ever make it through the entire list of pairs without making a switch, the SWITCH-OCCURRED flag will *not* have been set to "YES", meaning that no switch has occurred and that the array elements must already be in the correct order. This *might* be on the first or second pass through. If the array elements are already in the correct order at that point, there is no need to make more passes through the list. On the other hand, when a list starts out in the worst possible order, a switch needs to be made *every time through the list*. We'll stop making passes through the list when SWITCH-OCCURRED is "NO" after a complete trip through the array.

At the beginning of SORT-RECS, we have to initialize SWITCH-OCCURRED to "YES" to get into the comparison loop the first time. Note that SWITCH-OCCURRED is immediately set to "NO" and only gets set to "YES" again if and when a switch occurs.

With this improvement, we no longer need the variable Y, which was keeping track of the number of passes through the list. We just keep going through the list until no switches occur. For a list that starts out in order, we only go through the loop once. For a list that starts out in the *worst* possible order, switches will be made every time until PAIRS-TO-COMPARE has been reduced to 1. In this case, on the last pass through the loop, X is set to 1, SWITCH-OCCURRED is set to "NO", X equals PAIRS-TO-COMPARE, and the loop is exited. (See Figure 11.11.)

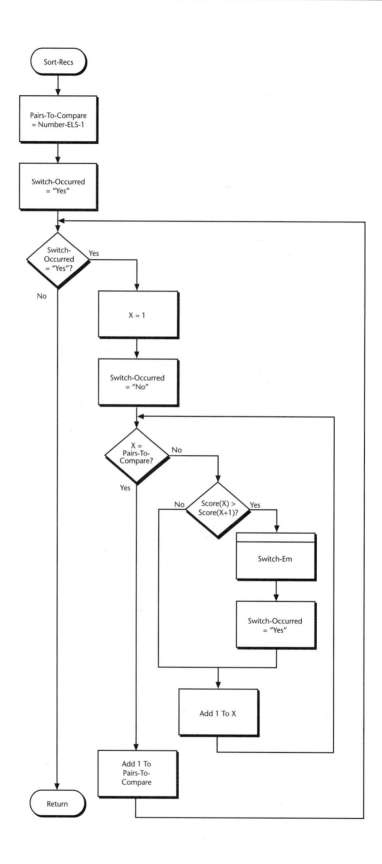

FIGURE 11.11

With these last two improvements, the program now makes just the number of comparisons it has to get the elements in the correct order.

Other Sorts

Insertion Sort

Even with the improvements, the bubble sort is actually one of the least efficient sorting methods available, but it works well and is easy for novice array users to understand and manipulate.

An **insertion sort** also looks at each pair of elements in an array until it finds one that is smaller than the one before it. This element is considered to be "out of order." As soon as such an element is located, the array is searched backward from that point to see where an element smaller than the "out of order" is located. At that point, the "out of order" element is *inserted* by moving each subsequent element down one.

For example, consider these scores:

SCORE(1) = 65
SCORE(2) = 80
SCORE(3) = 95
SCORE(4) = 75
SCORE(5) = 90

Using an insertion sort, 65 and 80 would be compared and left alone. The 80 and 95 would be compared and left alone. When 95 and 75 are compared, 75 would be determined to be "out of order."

Now, we would look backwards from the SCORE(4) of 75. SCORE(3) is not smaller, nor is SCORE(2); but since SCORE(1) is smaller than SCORE(4), SCORE(4) should follow it.

So, SCORE(4) would be stored in TEMP, SCORE(3), 95, would be moved to SCORE(4). SCORE(2), 80, would be moved to SCORE(3). Finally, TEMP, 75, would be placed in SCORE(2). The results:

SCORE(1) = 65
SCORE(2) = 75
SCORE(3) = 80
SCORE(4) = 95
SCORE(5) = 90

Comparisons would then continue on down the list.

The logic of the insertion sort is slightly more complicated than that for the bubble sort, but the insertion sort is more efficient because fewer "switches" are made.

Selection Sort

A **selection sort** is another sorting option. In a selection sort the first element in the array is assumed to be the smallest. Its value is stored in a variable we can call SMALLEST and its position in the array (1) is stored in a variable we can call POSITION. Then, every subsequent element in the array is tested. If one with a smaller value than SMALLEST is found, SMALLEST is set to the new value and POSITION is set to that element's position. After the entire array has been searched, SMALLEST will hold the smallest value and POSITION will hold its position.

The element originally in position 1 is then switched with the SMALLEST value, so at the end of the first pass through the array, the lowest value is in the first position, and the value that was in the first position is where the smallest value used to be.

For example, given:

SCORE(1) = 95
SCORE(2) = 80
SCORE(3) = 75
SCORE(4) = 65
SCORE(5) = 90

95 would be placed in SMALLEST. Then SCORE(2) would be checked. It's less than 95 so 2 would be placed in POSITION and 80 in SMALLEST. Then SCORE(3) would be tested. It's smaller than SMALLEST so 3 would be placed in POSITION and 75 in SMALLEST. SCORE(4) would be tested and since it is smaller than SMALLEST, 4 would be placed in POSITION and 65 in SMALLEST. SCORE(5) would be checked, but it isn't smaller than SMALLEST.

So at the end of the first pass, POSITION is 4 and SMALLEST is 65. 95 would be moved to SCORE(POSITION) and SMALLEST would be moved to SCORE(1) giving:

SCORE(1) = 65
SCORE(2) = 80
SCORE(3) = 75
SCORE(4) = 95
SCORE(5) = 90

Now that the smallest value is in the first position, the whole procedure would be repeated, starting with position 2. After the procedure has been repeated 1 less time than the number of elements being sorted, all elements will be in the correct order.

Again, with the selection sort, fewer switches are made than with the bubble sort, but the variables may be a little harder to keep track of.

Indexing

Sorting is not the most efficient method to use if a data file needs to be processed in order by one (or more) of the fields in each record. Many data files contain thousands of records, and sorting takes considerable time and computer memory.

Instead, records stored on a **random-access device**, such as a disk, are retrieved based on an **index**.

An index on a disk works much like the index in the back of a book. If you pick up a 400-page American history text because you need some facts about Betsy Ross, you would not want to start on page 1 and work your way through the text. Instead, you would turn to the index, discover Betsy Ross is located on page 218, and go directly to that page.

As pages in a book have numbers, locations on a disk or in memory, have **addresses**. In Chapter 2 we discussed the fact that every variable has an address in computer memory; likewise, every data record has an address at which it is stored. This is true whether we are talking about records on disk, or in computer memory.

Disks can have areas reserved for the index. Records can then be stored in any physical order on the disk, but the index can find the records in order based on specific fields.

For example, you might store employees on a disk in the order in which they are hired. Processing, however, often needs to take place in social security number order. As each new employee is added to such a file, the employee can physically be placed anywhere on the disk. Her social security number is inserted in proper order in the index, along with the physical **address** at which her record is located.

An index based on social security number might look like this:

Social Security Number	Location
111-22-3456	6400
222-44-7654	4800
333-55-1234	2400
444-88-9812	5200

Thus, even though a particular employee is hired last, and has the highest physical address on the disk, her low social security number will place her near the beginning of any ordered processing.

When a record is removed from an indexed file, it does not have to be physically removed. It can simply be deleted from the index, and thus will not be part of any further processing.

Linked Lists

Another way to access records in a desired order, even though they may not physically be stored in that order, is to create a **linked list**.

In its simplest form, a linked list involves creating one extra field in every record of stored data. This extra field holds the address of the record that should follow the current record.

For example, a record that was meant to store a customer's name, address, and phone number might contain the fields:

NAME
ADDRESS
PHONE-NUM
NEXT-ADDRESS

Every time a record is processed (printed, displayed, etc.), which particular record is processed next depends on the field NEXT-ADDRESS.

Every time a new record is added to a linked list, each existing record is examined until the proper logical location for the new record is located.

For example, let's assume that the customer records that need to be accessed in alphabetical order by name are stored as follows:

address of record	record NAME field	NEXT-ADDRESS
0000	ANDERSON	7200
7200	BENJAMIN	4400
4400	POOLE	6000
6000	ROGERS	EOF

You can see that each employee's record contains a NEXT-ADDRESS field that stores the address of the employee who follows alphabetically, even though that employee's record may physically be stored at a distant address.

If a new employee named ELLIS were hired, an available location would be found for ELLIS, perhaps 8400. Then the procedure would be:

1. ELLIS is compared with ANDERSON and found greater alphabetically, so the next employee is examined.

2. ELLIS is compared with BENJAMIN and found greater alphabetically, so the next employee is examined.

3. ELLIS is compared with POOLE and found lower alphabetically.

4. BENJAMIN's NEXT-ADDRESS is updated to ELLIS's address, 8400.

5. The NEXT-ADDRESS in ELLIS's record becomes 4400—the value that was previously stored in BENJAMIN'S NEXT-ADDRESS.

6. The new list becomes:

address of record	record NAME field	NEXT-ADDRESS
0000	ANDERSON	7200
7200	BENJAMIN	8400
8400	ELLIS	4400
4400	POOLE	6000
6000	ROGERS	EOF

As with indexing, when records are removed from a linked list, they do not need to be physically deleted. If POOLE was to be removed from the preceding list, all that would need to be done is to change ELLIS' NEXT-ADDRESS field to ROGERS' address: 6000. POOLE's record would then be bypassed during any further processing.

More sophisticated linked lists store *two* additional fields with each record. One field stores the address of the next record and the other field stores the address of the *previous* record so that the list may be accessed either forwards or backwards.

TERMS AND CONCEPTS

bubble sort
insertion sort
selection sort
random-access device
index
address
linked list

EXERCISES

 Exercise 1

Create the flowchart to read in a file of 10 employee salaries and print them out lowest to highest.

 Exercise 2

Create the flowchart to read in a file of 10 employee salaries and print them out highest to lowest.

Menus and Interactive Programming

Objectives

After studying Chapter 12, you should be able to:

- ▶ Define interactive programming.
- ▶ Design a menu system.
- ▶ Better understand the CASE structure.

Single-Level Menus

Many computer programs are run **interactively**. That is, they interact with the user changing the direction of the logic while they are running. A very common type of interactive program is a **menu** program in which the user is presented with a number of options on the screen and can select any one of them.

For example, an educational program that drills you on elementary arithmetic skills might have three options:

(1) Addition Problems
(2) Subtraction Problems
(3) Quit the Program

Please press a number to make your selection.

The final option, Quit the Program, is a very important one; without it there would be no elegant way for the program to terminate. It can be very frustrating to the user if this option is left off a menu.

Some menu programs require the user to enter a number to choose a menu option, for example, a 2 to perform a subtraction drill from the preceding menu. Other menu programs require the user to enter a letter of the alphabet, for example, an S for a subtraction drill. Other programs allow the user to use a pointing device such as a mouse or the keyboard arrow keys to point to a choice on the screen to make a selection. The most sophisticated programs allow the user to employ whichever of those selection methods is most convenient at the time.

Let's start by writing a simple program that only allows the user to enter a digit to make a choice. The main logic for an interactive menu program need not be substantially different from any of the other sequential file programs we've discussed so far in this book. There is a START-UP subroutine, a LOOPING subroutine, and a CLEAN-UP subroutine.

The main control of a menu program, however, is not the EOF? question. The EOF? question is appropriate when a file of records is being read and processed but a menu program's end is not controlled by an end of file condition; rather it is controlled by a user's menu response. Our main line logic, then, will be controlled by the question: RESPONSE = 3?. (See Figure 12.1.)

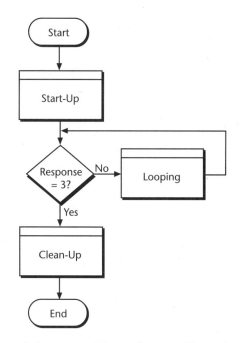

FIGURE 12.1

The START-UP routine defines variables and opens files. The manner in which the files are opened, which depends on the programming language you will eventually use, lets the program know that subsequent **WRITE** statements will go to the screen and **READ** statements will accept data from the keyboard. It also displays the menu for the first time so that the user can make a choice. (See Figure 12.2.)

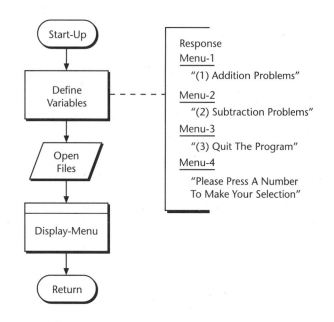

FIGURE 12.2

The display of the menu has been placed in its own subroutine, DISPLAY-MENU, for convenience. DISPLAY-MENU writes the four lines of the menu to the screen, and then the READ RESPONSE statement reads in a number from the keyboard.

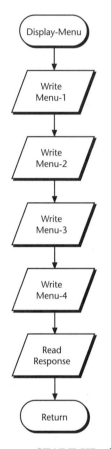

FIGURE 12.3

When the logic of the program leaves START-UP, there is a RESPONSE waiting in memory to be processed. If the RESPONSE is not a 3, for the Quit the Program option, the program enters the LOOPING routine. The LOOPING routine performs one of two subroutines, ADDITION or SUBTRACTION, based on the user's input. Whichever type of arithmetic drill is performed, the DISPLAY-MENU routine is called again, and the user has the opportunity to select the same arithmetic drill, a different one, or the Quit the Program option. (See Figure 12.4.)

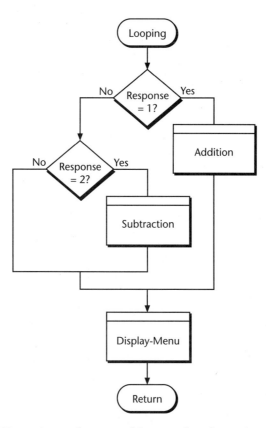

FIGURE 12.4

When the LOOPING routine ends, control is passed to the main program. If the user has selected the Quit the Program option during the **DISPLAY-MENU** routine, the question RESPONSE=3? sends the program to the CLEAN-UP routine. That routine simply closes the files, as shown in Figure 12.5.

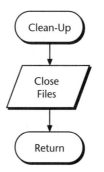

FIGURE 12.5

At the end of LOOPING, when the menu is displayed, if the user selects anything *other than* 3, LOOPING is entered again. Note that if the user chooses 4 or 9 or any other invalid menu item, the menu is simply displayed again. Unfortunately the user may be confused by the repeated display of the menu. Perhaps the user is familiar with another program in which option 9 has always meant Quit. When using this program, the user who does not read the menu carefully may press 9, get the menu back, press 9, and get the menu back again. The programmer can assist the user by displaying a message when the selected RESPONSE is not one of the allowable menu options. (See Figure 12.6.)

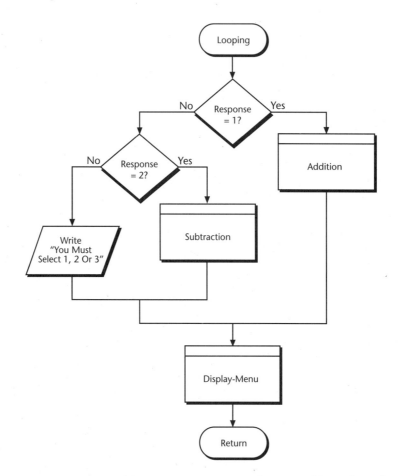

FIGURE 12.6

A program to use a menu with more numerous options would not be substantially different from a program with three options. More decisions would be made and additional subroutines would be performed, as shown in Figure 12.7.

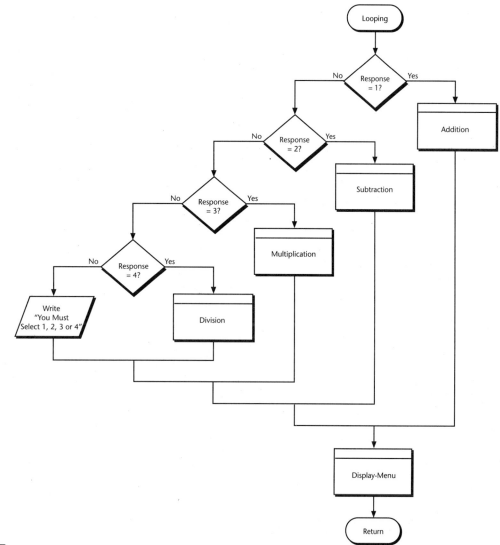

FIGURE 12.7

The CASE structure (see Chapter 3) can become extremely convenient in a situation like this as an alternative to a long series of decisions. But the CASE structure is never actually necessary; a series of decisions will do the job. The syntax of CASE structures in most programming languages allows an Other or **default option** if none of the specified cases is true. In this instance, our default is an error message if none of the cases 1 through 4 has occurred. (See Figure 12.8.)

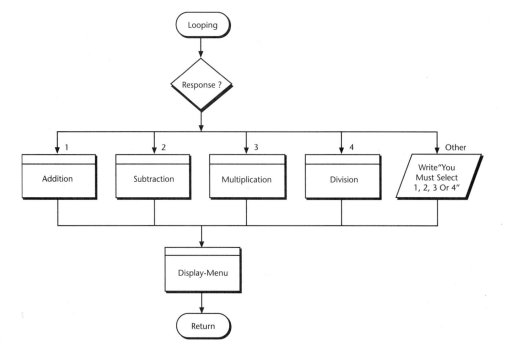

FIGURE 12.8

Our menu program could be improved upon by allowing letters of the alphabet as well as numeric responses to select options. One change in the logic would be to make sure RESPONSE was defined as a character variable capable of holding alphabetic characters. This is done differently in different languages. The only other change would be that many more "legal" menu RESPONSEs would exist.

One subtlety often overlooked by novice programmers is that computers recognize capital letters as completely unique from their lowercase counterparts. A good menu program then would allow three responses for the (1) Addition option: "1", "A", and "a".

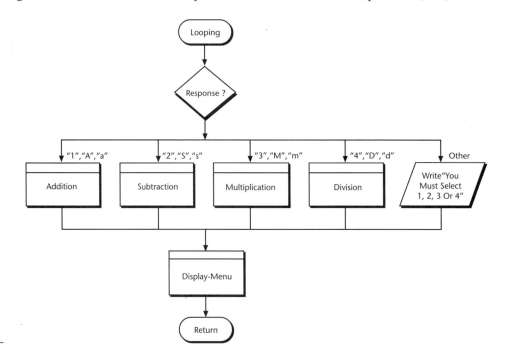

FIGURE 12.9

Multilevel Menus

Sometimes a program requires more options than can easily fit in one menu. This poses three potential problems:

1. Not all the options will appear on the screen.
2. The screen is too crowded to be visually pleasing.
3. The user is confused by too many choices.

In these cases, **multilevel menus** may be more effective. With a multi-level menu, the selection of a menu option leads to another menu.

For example, if the Arithmetic Drill program had three levels of Addition problems:

(1) Easy
(2) Medium
(3) Difficult
(4) Quit this menu

then these four options might come up only if (1) Addition was selected off the main menu.

The ADDITION subroutine might then appear as shown in Figure 12.10, and ADDITION-OPTIONS might appear as shown in Figure 12.11.

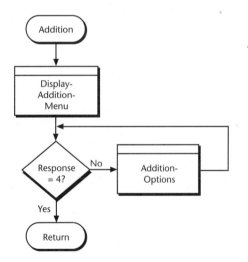

FIGURE 12.10

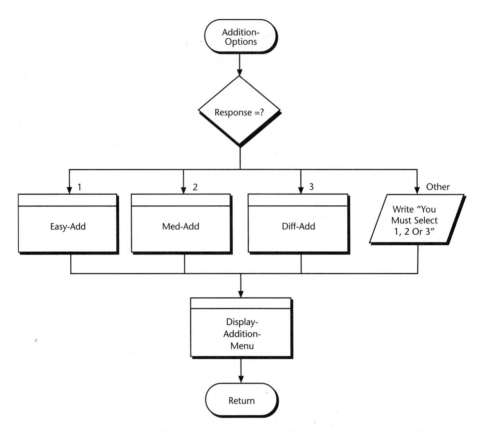

FIGURE 12.11

If (1) Addition is selected from the main menu, the ADDITION routine displays its own menu with the (1) Easy, (2) Medium, (3) Difficult, (4) Quit this menu choices. If the user response is 4, control passes out of the ADDITION routine and back to the main menu. If the user response is other than 4, ADDITION-OPTIONS calls the appropriate routines or writes an error message.

The last task in ADDITION-OPTIONS is to display the ADDITION menu again. If anything other than 4 is chosen, ADDITION-OPTIONS is performed again.

Many programs have several levels of menus. The EASY-ADD routine could display a new menu asking the user if she wanted:

(1) Short quiz
(2) Regular test
(3) Final exam
(4) Quit this menu

No new techniques would be needed to create as many levels of menus as the application warrants.

TERMS AND CONCEPTS

interactive programming
menu
default option

EXERCISES

Exercise 1

Suggest two subsequent levels of menus for each of the first two options in this main menu:

(1) Print records from file
(2) Delete records from file
(3) Quit

Exercise 2

Draw the logic for a program that gives you the following options:

(1) Hot dog   *1.50*
(2) Fries   *1.00*
(3) Lemonade   *.75*
(4) End order

You should be allowed to keep ordering from the menu until you press (4) End order, at which point you should see a total amount due for your entire order.

Exercise 3

Draw the logic for a program that displays the rules for

(1) Sports
(2) Games
(3) Quit

If the user chooses (1) Sports, display options for four different sports of your choice. If the user chooses (2) Games, display options for

(1) Card games
(2) Board games
(3) Quit

Display options for at least two card games and two board games of your choice.

Sequential File Merging, Matching, and Updating

Objectives

After studying Chapter 13, you should be able to:

▲ Explain the concept of a sequential file.

▲ Explain the difference between a master and a transaction file.

▲ Describe the steps to merging, matching, and updating sequential files.

Merging

A **sequential file** is a file whose records are stored one after another in some order. A sequential file of your friends might simply be stored in the order in which you met these friends—your best friend from kindergarten is record 1 and the friend you just made last week is record 30.

Often, however, the order of the records is based on one or more of the fields in each record. Perhaps it is most useful for you to store your friends sequentially in alphabetical order by last name, or maybe in order by birthday.

Other examples of sequential files would be a file of parts records for a manufacturing company stored in order by part number, a file of customers for a business in order by zip code, or a file of employees in order of social security number.

It is a very common occurrence in business to have two or more files that need to be **merged** together. For example, you might have one file of current employees in social security number order and another file of newly hired employees also in social security number order. You need to merge these two files into one big file before running this week's payroll program.

Another common example would be to have a list of customers from the East Coast office in alphabetical order and a list of customers from the West Coast office in alphabetical order. You might wish to make one list of the entire company's customers in alphabetical order.

Let's assume that those two customer files exist. The fields in each file are NAME and BALANCE. For reference, we can call the fields in the East Coast file EAST-NAME and EAST-BALANCE and the fields in the West Coast file WEST-NAME and WEST-BALANCE. Of course, any names for these fields would be fine as long as they are one word and have some meaning.

The following data is contained in the files:

East Coast File

EAST-NAME	EAST-BALANCE
Adams	100.00
Brown	50.00
Davis	25.00
Harris	300.00
Ingram	400.00
Johns	30.00

West Coast File

WEST-NAME	WEST-BALANCE
Cass	200.00
Ellis	125.00
Fell	75.00
Grand	100.00

The desired merged file would look like this:

Entire Company File

MERGED-NAME	MERGED-BALANCE
Adams	100.00
Brown	50.00
Cass	200.00
Davis	25.00
Ellis	125.00

Fell	75.00
Grand	100.00
Harris	300.00
Ingram	400.00
Johns	30.00

The main logic for this type of program is the same main logic we've seen over and over before: a HOUSEKEEPING routine, a MAIN-LOOP, and a FINISH-UP.

In HOUSEKEEPING, however, for the first time we need to define two input files. We're calling them EAST-FILE and WEST-FILE. Their variable fields are EAST-NAME, EAST-BALANCE, WEST-NAME, and WEST-BALANCE, respectively.

No printing is done in this program because the output is simply going to be a merged file with the same format as the two input files. In most programming languages, there is no special trick to writing to a file instead of to the printer; it's simply that when writing the OPEN FILES statement in HOUSEKEEPING, a disk file is named rather than the printer. The command verb to send output to the appropriate device is usually the same. We've usually been using the verb *write* to indicate output, and we will continue to do so here.

The rest of HOUSEKEEPING is pretty straightforward. (See Figure 13.1.) Instead of the usual last event of HOUSEKEEPING being to read the first record into memory, the last event of HOUSEKEEPING is to read the first record from *each file* into memory.

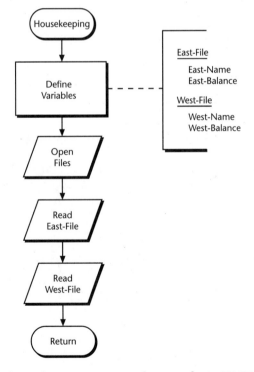

FIGURE 13.1

When the MAIN-LOOP is begun, two records—one from EAST-FILE and one from WEST-FILE—are sitting in the memory of the computer. One of these records needs to be written to the new output file first. Which one? It depends on which one has the lesser value alphabetically. So MAIN-LOOP begins like Figure 13.2.

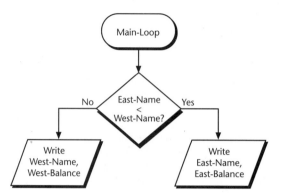

FIGURE 13.2

Using the data just given for an example, the record of Adams would be written to the output file while Cass's record waits in memory because the EAST-NAME, "Adams," is alphabetically less than the WEST-NAME, "Cass."

Should Cass's record be written to the output file next? Not necessarily. It depends on who is next after Adams on the EAST-FILE. We need to read that record in and compare it to "Cass." Since, in this case, the next record on the EAST-FILE is "Brown," another record from the EAST-FILE is written to output.

Is it Cass's turn to be written now? You really don't know until you read another record from the EAST-FILE and compare. Since this one is "Davis," it is indeed time to write Cass. After Cass is written to output, should you now write Davis? You don't know until you read the next record from the WEST-FILE to see if that one should be placed prior to or after placing Davis.

So, the MAIN-LOOP proceeds like this: compare two records; write the lower record out, and read another record from the *same* input file. (See Figure 13.3.)

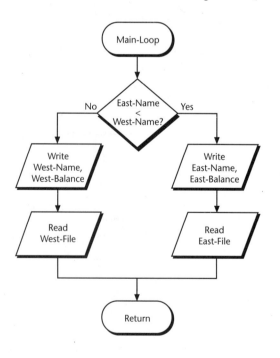

FIGURE 13.3

If you recall the two original files:

East Coast File

EAST-NAME	EAST-BALANCE
Adams	100.00
Brown	50.00
Davis	25.00
Harris	300.00
Ingram	400.00
Johns	30.00

West Coast File

WEST-NAME	WEST-BALANCE
Cass	200.00
Ellis	125.00
Fell	75.00
Grand	100.00

here's what happens:

1. Adams and Cass are compared, Adams written out, and Brown read.
2. Brown and Cass are compared, Brown written out, and Davis read.
3. Davis and Cass are compared, Cass written out, and Ellis read.
4. Davis and Ellis are compared, Davis written out and Harris read.
5. Harris and Ellis are compared, Ellis written out, and Fell read.
6. Harris and Fell are compared, Fell written out, and Grand read.
7. Harris and Grand are compared, Grand written out, and end of file is encountered.

What happens now? Is the program over? It shouldn't be because Harris, Ingram, and Johns all need to be included on the new output file and none of them has been written yet. But if we read in a record from one of the files and EOF is encountered, the main line EOF? question sends us to the FINISH-UP routine. How do we get the rest of the records off the EAST-FILE?

The solution involves creating a new **flag** variable that we can call BOTH-AT-EOF. At the beginning of the program, we can set BOTH-AT-EOF to a value of "NO". Only when both the EAST-FILE *and* the WEST-FILE are at EOF will we store a value of "YES" in the BOTH-AT-EOF field. (See Figure 13.4.)

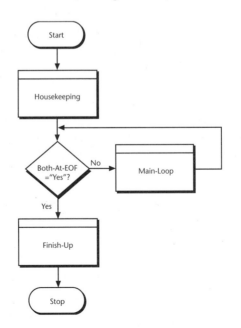

FIGURE 13.4

Every time we read the WEST-FILE, we can check for EOF. When EOF occurs, set the field that is being compared, in this case, WEST-NAME, to a very high value. "ZZZ" is an example of a very high value, and it's safe to say it is probably higher than the name of anybody on either of our files. Similarly, when reading the EAST-FILE, set EAST-NAME to "ZZZ" when EOF occurs. When *both* EAST-NAME *and* WEST-NAME are "ZZZ", then BOTH-AT-EOF can be set to "YES".

In our example, when WEST-FILE is read, EOF is encountered and WEST-NAME gets set to "ZZZ". Now, when MAIN-LOOP is entered again, EAST-NAME and WEST-NAME are compared and EAST-NAME is still "Harris". EAST-NAME ("Harris") is therefore *less* than WEST-NAME ("ZZZ"). The data for EAST-NAME's record is written to the output, and another EAST-FILE record is read. The original files again are:

East Coast File   West Coast File

EAST-NAME	EAST-BALANCE	WEST-NAME	WEST-BALANCE
Adams	100.00	Cass	200.00
Brown	50.00	Ellis	125.00
Davis	25.00	Fell	75.00
Harris	300.00	Grand	100.00
Ingram	400.00		
Johns	30.00		

The complete run now proceeds like this:

1. Adams and Cass are compared, Adams written out, and Brown read.
2. Brown and Cass are compared, Brown written out, and Davis read.
3. Davis and Cass are compared, Cass written out, and Ellis read.
4. Davis and Ellis are compared, Davis written out and Harris read.
5. Harris and Ellis are compared, Ellis written out, and Fell read.
6. Harris and Fell are compared, Fell written out, and Grand read.
7. Harris and Grand are compared, Grand written out, end of file encountered, and ZZZ moved to WEST-NAME.
8. Harris and ZZZ are compared, Harris written out, and Ingram read.
9. Ingram and ZZZ are compared, Ingram written out, and Johns read.
10. Johns and ZZZ are compared, Johns written out, end of file encountered on the EAST-COAST-FILE, and ZZZ moved to EAST-NAME.
11. Now that both names are ZZZ, set the flag BOTH-AT-EOF equal to "YES".

The BOTH-AT-EOF flag must originally be set to "NO" (or any other value you choose *other than* "YES") in the HOUSEKEEPING section. Only when both the EAST-FILE and the WEST-FILE have reached EOF will the BOTH-AT-EOF flag be changed to a value of "YES".

Figure 13.5 shows the completed MAIN-LOOP.

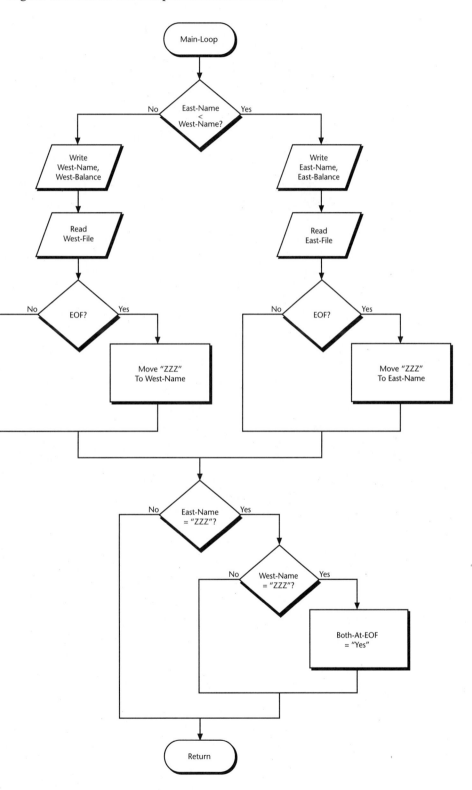

 FIGURE 13.5

Matching

Besides merging files, another common operation with sequential files is **matching**. For example, I could have a file of customers for my business with fields such as CUST-NUMBER, CUST-NAME, CUST-ADDRESS, CUST-PHONE, and CUST-SALES-VOLUME. This file could be called a **master file**.

CUSTOMER MASTER FILE DESCRIPTION

FILE NAME: CUST-REC

FIELD NAME	POSITIONS	DATA TYPE	DECIMALS
CUST-NUMBER	*1–3*	*Numeric*	*0*
CUST-NAME	*4–23*	*Character*	
CUST-ADDRESS	*24–43*	*Character*	
CUST-PHONE	*44–53*	*Numeric*	*0*
CUST-SALES-VOLUME	*54–60*	*Numeric*	*2*

Periodically, perhaps at the end of each day, or maybe not until the end of the week, I would want to update the CUST-SALES-VOLUME field with any new sales transactions that occurred in that time period. Therefore, I always have a running total of how much that customer has purchased from me. To this end, I may have created a **transaction file**. This transaction file would have one record in it for every transaction that has occurred. The fields in the transaction file would be a customer number, the date of the transaction, and the amount. I could call these TRANS-CUST-NUMBER, TRANS-DATE, and TRANS-AMOUNT.

TRANSACTION FILE DESCRIPTION

FILE NAME: TRANS-REC

FIELD NAME	POSITIONS	DATA TYPE	DECIMALS
TRANS-CUST-NUMBER	*1–3*	*Numeric*	*0*
TRANS-DATE	*4–9*	*Numeric*	*0*
TRANS-AMOUNT	*10–17*	*Numeric*	*2*

What I wish to create is a new master file on which almost all the information is the same as on the original file, but the CUST-SALES-VOLUME field has been increased to reflect the most recent transaction.

What I will need to do is go through the old master file one record at a time, and see if there is a new sale for that customer. If there are no transactions for a customer, the new customer record will contain exactly the same information as the old customer record. If, however, there was a transaction for a customer, the **TRANS-AMOUNT** should be added to the **CUST-SALES-VOLUME** field before writing the record to output.

HOUSEKEEPING here looks very similar to the HOUSEKEEPING routine in the file-merging program. Two records are read, one from the master file and one from the transaction file. Two read routines are created, each storing a high value in the customer number fields when EOF is encountered. (In the file-merging program, we used "ZZZ" because character fields (customer names) were being compared. In this example, numeric fields (customer numbers) are being used, so we'll store the highest numeric value for a three-digit number, 999. (See Figures 13.6, 13.7, and 13.8.)

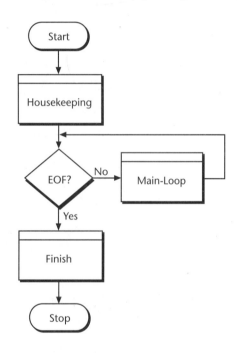

FIGURE 13.6

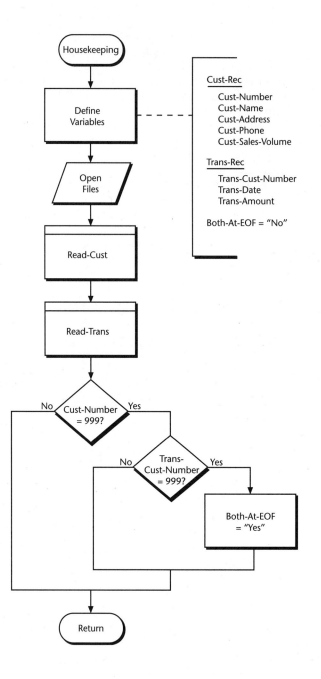

 FIGURE 13.7

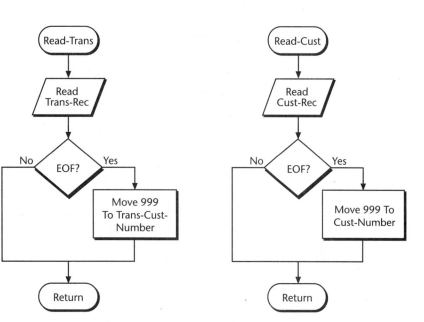

FIGURE 13.8

In the merging program, the first thing we had to do in MAIN-LOOP was determine which file held the lower value record and write that file to output. In a matching program, we need to determine more than whether or not one file's **key field** is larger than another's; it's also important to know whether or not they are equal. (See Figure 13.9.)

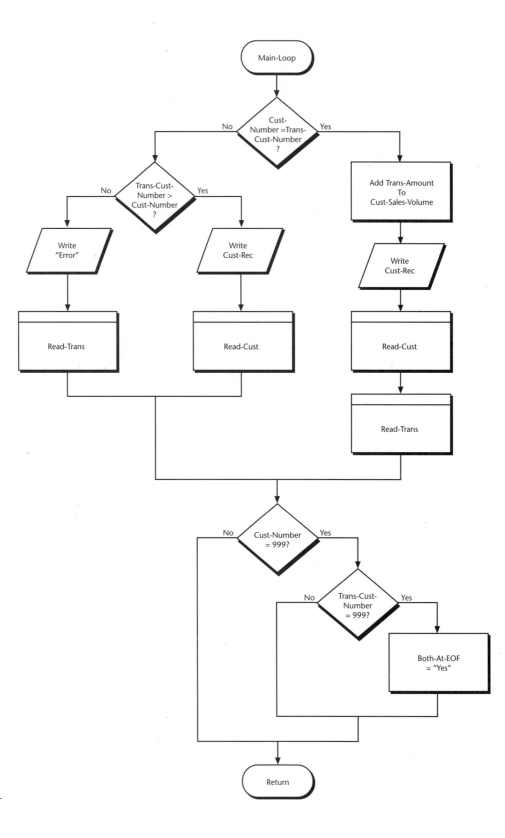

FIGURE 13.9

So now, in MAIN-LOOP, the CUST-NUMBER and the TRANS-CUST-NUMBER are compared. If they are equal, the TRANS-AMOUNT is added to the CUST-SALES-VOLUME, the updated master record is written to output, and both a new master record and a new transaction record can be read.

If, however, the TRANS-CUST-NUMBER is higher than the CUST-NUMBER, that means there wasn't a sale for that customer. That's all right. Just write the original customer record to output exactly the same way it came in on input; then get the next customer record to see if this is the one the transaction pertains to.

Finally, if the TRANS-CUST-NUMBER is less than the CUST-NUMBER on the master file, that means you're trying to record a transaction for which no master record exists. That must be an error; a transaction should always have a master record. Perhaps you should write an error message to an output device, such as the printer, before reading the next transaction record. At the bottom of the MAIN-LOOP then, after a new master record or transaction record or both have been read, if both CUST-NUMBER and TRANS-CUST-NUMBER are 999, it's time to set the BOTH-AT-EOF flag to "YES".

Walk through the problem with this sample data:

Master File		Transaction File	
CUST-NUMBER	CUST-SALES-VOLUME	TRANS-CUST-NUMBER	TRANS-SALES-AMOUNT
100	1000.00	100	400.00
102	50.00	105	700.00
103	500.00	108	100.00
105	75.00	110	400.00
106	5000.00		
109	4000.00		
110	500.00		

The program would proceed like this:

1. Cust 100 is read from the master file and cust 100 is read from the transaction file. They are equal, so 400.00 is added to 1000.00 and a new master file record is written out with a 1400.00 volume figure. A new record is read from each file.

2. Now master is 102 and transaction is 105, so there are no transactions today for customer 102. Write out the master just the way it came in and get a new master.

3. Now master is 103 and transaction is 105. Write out the master as is and get a new one.

4. Now master is 105 and transaction is 105. The new sales volume figure is 775.00 and a new master record is written out. Read one record from each file.

5. Now master is 106 and transaction is 108. Write out customer record 106 as it was coming in and read another master.

6. Now master is 109 and transaction is 108. An error has occurred. We are saying we sold something to customer 108, but there is no record of a customer number 108, so a human had better be alerted. Write an error message on the printer, and get a new transaction record.

7. Now master is 109 and transaction is 110. Write out master record 109 and get a new one.

8. Now master is 100 and transaction is 110. Add the 400.00 transaction to the previous 500.00 figure and write out a new record with a 900.00 figure in it. Read one record from each file.

9. Since both files are done, end the job.

Updating

In the example just discussed, a master file needed to have some of its records updated with new figures, and this would be a common occurrence in what data processors know as an **update program**. A good update program, however, should also be able to add new customers into the master file and, conversely, remove old customers who are not active any more.

Assume you have an employee file with fields like EMP-NUM, EMP-NAME, EMP-SALARY, and EMP-DEPT. Sometimes a new employee is hired and needs to be added to this file, or an employee quits and needs to be removed from the file. Sometimes a change needs to be made to an employee record, for example, a raise in salary or a change of department.

For this kind of program, it's common to have a transaction file that has all the same fields as the master file, with one exception. The transaction file would have one extra field to indicate whether this transaction is meant to be an add, a delete, or a change—maybe a one-letter code of "A", "D", or "C".

A typical ADD record on the transaction file would have the code "A" and all the rest of the fields, TRANS-NUM, TRANS-NAME, TRANS-SALARY, TRANS-DEPT, and so on, filled in. This is a new employee, and all data needs to be entered for him or her for the first time.

A typical DELETE record really only needs the "D" code and the TRANS-NUM. If the TRANS-NUM matches an EMP-NUM on a master record, that's the record you want to delete. Why bother typing in the salary, department, or anything else for someone you're getting rid of?

A typical CHANGE record needs the "C" code and needs data only in the fields that are going to be changed. In other words, if an employee's salary is staying the same, leave the TRANS-SALARY field blank; but if her department is changing from 12 to 28, fill in a 28 in the department field of the transaction record.

The main line of an update program looks the same as the merging and matching programs we have written. (See Figure 13.10.)

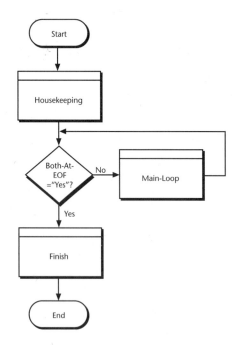

FIGURE 13.10

HOUSEKEEPING defines the variables, opens the files, and reads the first record from each file. As in the merging program, we create routines to read each of the input files. The key fields, EMP-NUM and TRANS-NUM, are set to very high values at EOF. (See Figures 13.11 and 13.12.)

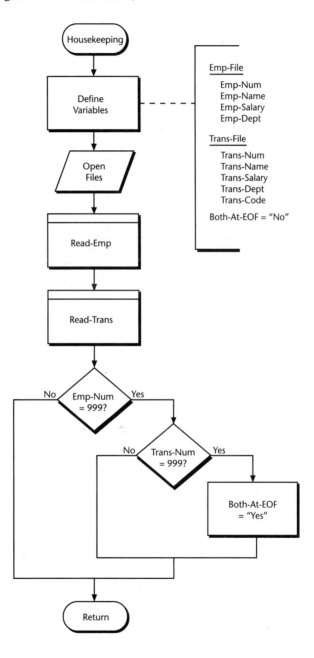

FIGURE 13.11

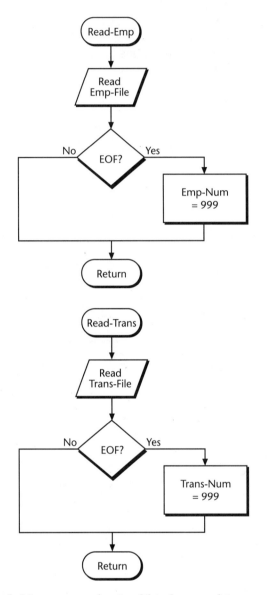

FIGURE 13.12

The MAIN-LOOP of this program begins like the matching program. We need to know if the EMP-NUM on the master file and the TRANS-NUM on the transaction file are equal or if EMP-NUM is higher, or if TRANS-NUM is higher.

To keep the MAIN-LOOP simple, we'll have each of these three situations perform a different subroutine. We'll call them THEY-ARE-EQUAL, EMP-IS-LARGER-THAN-TRANS, and TRANS-IS-LARGER-THAN-EMP. Of course, you might choose shorter subroutine names, but these long subroutine names should help us keep in mind here which field was larger. At the end of MAIN-LOOP, we'll set the BOTH-AT-EOF flag to "YES" if both files have completed. (See Figure 13.13.)

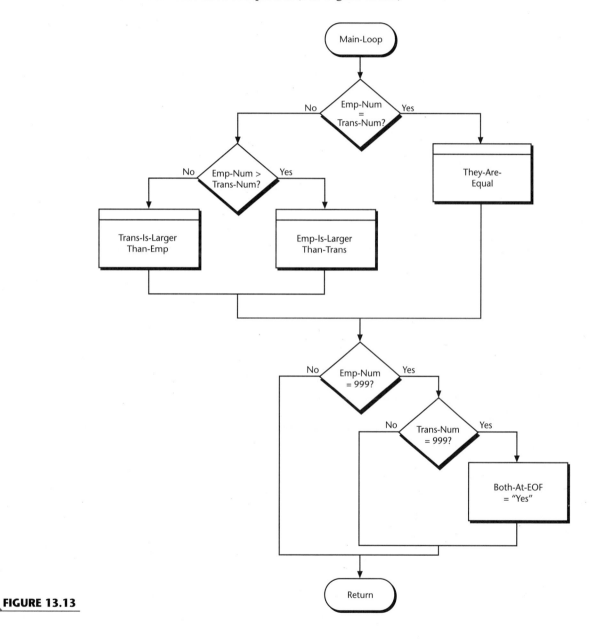

FIGURE 13.13

The THEY-ARE-EQUAL subroutine is entered only if a record on the master file and a record on the transaction file have the same employee number. This should be the situation when a change, like a new salary, is being made to a record, or when a record needs to be deleted.

What if the master file and the transaction file records are equal, but the TRANS-CODE on the transaction record is an "A"? If so, an error situation has occurred. You should not be attempting to add an employee who already exists in our file.

THEY-ARE-EQUAL, then, checks the TRANS-CODE and performs one of three actions:

1. If the code is an "A", an error message is printed. Since we're not really sure what the error is (Is the code wrong? Was this meant to be a change or a delete of an existing employee? Or is the employee number wrong and this was meant to be the add of some new employee?), we should print out an error message of some sort to let a human know an error situation has occurred. We should also write the existing master record to output exactly the same way it came in without making any changes.

2. If the code is a "C", changes need to be made. Each field on the transaction record should be checked. If any field is blank, the data on the new master record should come from the old master record. If, however, a field on the transaction record contains data, this data is intended to be a change. The corresponding field on the new master record should come from the transaction record. For all changed fields then, we replace the contents of the old field on the master file with the new value in the corresponding field on the transaction file. Then we write out the record.

3. If the code is not an "A" or a "C", it must be a "D" and the record should be deleted. How do you delete a record from a new master file? Just don't write it there in the first place!

To keep our illustration simple here, we are assuming that all the transaction records have been checked by a previous program and all TRANS-CODEs are "A", "C", or "D". If this were not the case, we would simply add one more decision to the THEY-ARE-EQUAL routine. If the TRANS-CODE is not "C", ask if it is "D". If so, delete the record; if not, it must not be "A", "C", or "D", so write an error message.

Finally, in the THEY-ARE-EQUAL routine, if the master file record and the trans-action file record have matched and been dealt with, one new record needs to be read from each of the two files. (See Figure 13.14.)

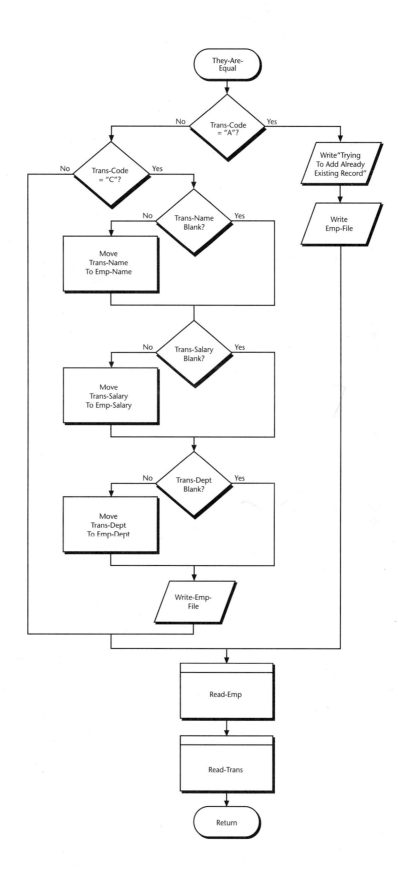

 **FIGURE 13.14**

Suppose, in the MAIN-LOOP, the master file record and the transaction file record do *not* match. Perhaps the master record has a larger employee number than the transaction file record. If the EMP-IS-LARGER-THAN-TRANS subroutine is entered, a transaction record has been read for which there is no master record.

If the transaction record is a code "A", that's fine since an add shouldn't have a master record. The transaction record simply becomes the new master record and is written to the new output file.

If, however, the code is "C" or "D", an error has occurred. You are attempting to make a change to a nonexistent record or you are attempting to delete a nonexistent record. Either way, a mistake has been made. An error message must be printed.

At the end of the EMP-IS-LARGER-THAN-TRANS routine, another master record should not be read. After all, there could be several more transactions that are adds before a master record matches or is less than a transaction. Therefore, only a transaction record should be read. (See Figure 13.15.)

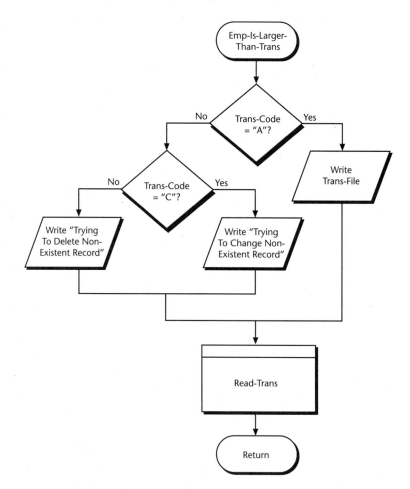

FIGURE 13.15

The last possibility in the MAIN-LOOP is that a master file record is smaller than the transaction file record in memory. If the TRANS-IS-LARGER-THAN-EMP subroutine is entered, there is no transaction for a given master file record. What could be simpler? There is a master record for which there are no changes and no deletions (and no mistake of trying to add it in when it already exists). So, just write the new master record out exactly like the old master record, and read another master record. (See Figure 13.16.)

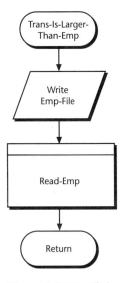

FIGURE 13.16

At some point, one of the files will reach EOF. If the transaction file reaches the end first, TRANS-NUM is set to 999 in the READ-TRANS routine. Each time MAIN-LOOP is entered after TRANS-NUM is set to 999, EMP-NUM will be less than TRANS-NUM. The TRANS-IS-LARGER-THAN-EMP routine will be performed. That's the routine that writes out records from the master file in exactly the same way as they came in. This is exactly what you want to have happen. There obviously were no transactions for these final records on the master file because the transactions have already all been used up.

If, on the other hand, the master file reaches the end first, EMP-NUM is set to 999 in the READ-EMP routine. Now, each time MAIN-LOOP is entered, the TRANS-NUM will be less than the EMP-NUM for all remaining records. The EMP-IS-LARGER-THAN-TRANS routine is the one that will be performed. The transactions at the end of the transaction file will be checked. If they are adds, they will be written to the new master as new records. However, if they are changes or deletions, a mistake has been made because there are no corresponding master file records.

Whichever file reaches the end first, the other continues to be read from and processed. When that file reaches EOF, the BOTH-AT-EOF flag will finally be set to "YES". Then FINISH can be performed, as shown in Figure 13.17.

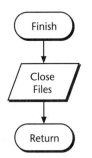

FIGURE 13.17

TERMS AND CONCEPTS

sequential file
merging
matching
updating
master file
transaction file
BOTH-AT-EOF flag

EXERCISES

ex. *Exercise 1*

You run a talent agency that books bands for social functions. You maintain a master file in the following format:

TALENT FILE DESCRIPTION

FILE NAME: BANDS

FIELD CONTENTS	POSITIONS	DATA TYPE	DECIMALS	EXAMPLE
Band code	1–3	Numeric	0	176
Band name	4–33	Character		The Polka Pals
Contact person	34–53	Character		Jay Sakowicz
Phone	54–63	Numeric	0	8154556012
Style	64–71	Character		Polka
Hourly rate	72–76	Numeric	2	07500

Occasionally changes have to be made to the file. Transaction records are made with the same format as the master records just described plus one additional field that holds a transaction code, which is "A" if you are adding a new band to the file, "C" if you are changing some of the data in an existing file, and "D" if you are deleting a band from the file.

An "add" transaction record contains a band code, an "A" in the transaction code field, and all of the rest of the fields are filled in with the new band's data. During processing, an error can occur if you attempt to add a band code that already exists on the file. This is not allowed, and an error message is printed.

A "change" transaction record contains a band code, a "C" in the transaction code field, and only those fields that are changing are filled in. For example, a band that is raising its hourly rate from $75 to $100 per hour would have the band name field, contact person information, and style of music blank on the transaction record, but the hourly rate field would contain 100. During processing, an error can occur if you are attempting to change data for a band number that doesn't exist on the master file. An error message is printed.

A "delete" transaction record contains a band code, a "D" in the transaction code field, and no other data. During processing, an error can occur if you are attempting to delete a band number that doesn't exist on the master file. An error message is printed.

Two forms of output are created. One is the new updated master file with all changes, additions, and deletions. The other is a printed report of errors that occurred during processing. Rather than just a list of error messages, each line of the printed output should list the appropriate BAND-CODE, along with the corresponding message.

Design the print chart for the error report, and the hierarchy chart and flowchart for the program.

Appendix A

Consider the flowchart segment in Figure A.1. Is it structured?

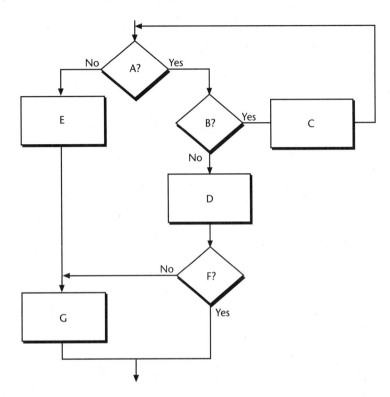

FIGURE A.1

No, it's not. Let's straighten it out. We'll use the "spaghetti" method. Start with A. This must be the beginning of either a selection or a loop. (See Figure A.2.)

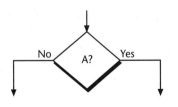

FIGURE A.2

Let's tackle the left side A first. Pull up on the left branch of the decision and you get E, followed by G, followed by the end. (See Figure A.3.)

Now pull up on the right side. A decision symbol, B, comes up. Pull on B's left side, and a process, D, comes up next. (See Figure A.4.)

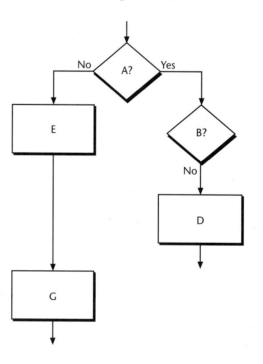

After D, a decision F comes up. Pull on its left side and get a process, G, then the end. Pull on F's right side and simply reach the end. (See Figure A.5.)

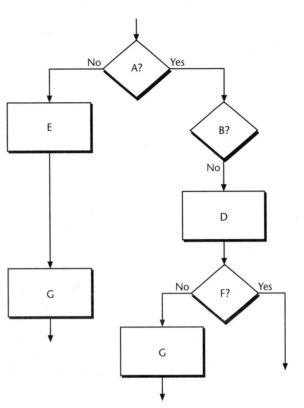

The big problem with the original flowchart segment lies on the right side of the B decision. Pull up and get C. This looks like a loop because it doubles back on itself, up to decision A. However, the rules of a structured loop say that it must have this appearance: a question, followed by a structure, returning right back to the question. If the arrow coming out of C returned right to B, there would be no problem, but the question A must be repeated. The spaghetti technique says if things are tangled up, start repeating. So bring another A decision down after C. (See Figure A.6.)

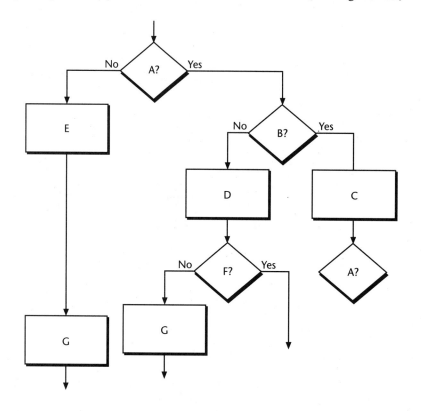

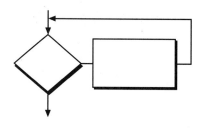

A Structured Loop

 FIGURE A.6

Now, on the right side of A, B repeats. On the right side of B, C repeats. After C, A occurs. On the right side of A, B occurs. On the right side of B, C occurs. After C, A occurs again. Are you getting the picture that we'll *never* get out of this? (See Figure A.7.)

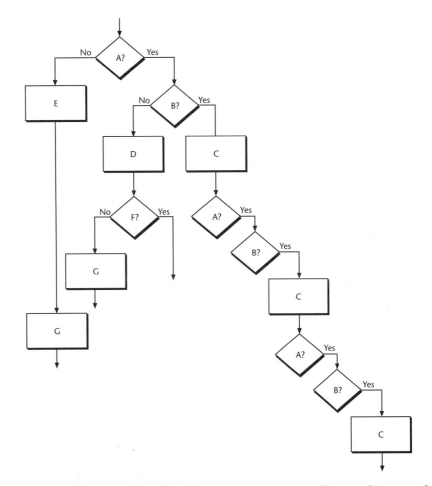

FIGURE A.7

Sometimes, in order to make a flowchart segment structured, something new has to be added to it. An extra variable, sometimes known as a flag, can get us out of this endless mess.

We'll create a flag called GO-BACK-TO-A and we'll set the value of GO-BACK-TO-A to "YES" or "NO", depending on whether we want to go back to A. Figure A.8 shows the original flowchart segment again.

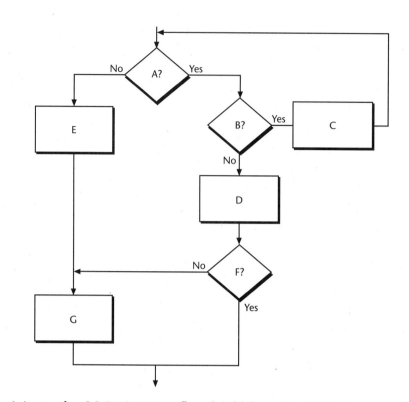

FIGURE A.8

When A is no, the GO-BACK-TO-A flag should be set to "NO" because when A is "NO", we never want to go back to the question A again. (See Figure A.9.)

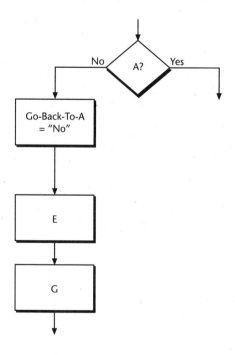

FIGURE A.9

Similarly, when B is no, we never want to go back to A again either. (See Figure A.10.)

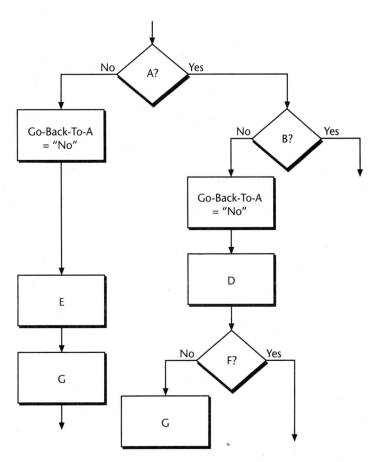

When B is yes, however, we do want to go back to A. So when B is yes, perform process C and set the GO-BACK-TO-A flag equal to "YES". (See Figure A.11.)

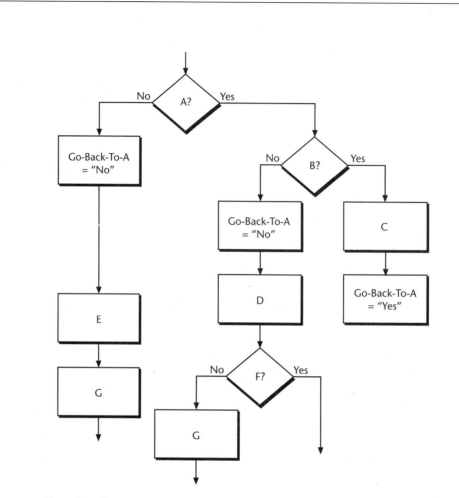

Now, all paths of the flowchart can come together at the bottom with one final question: Is GO-BACK-TO-A equal to "YES"? If it isn't, exit; but if it is, go back to A! (See Figure A.12.)

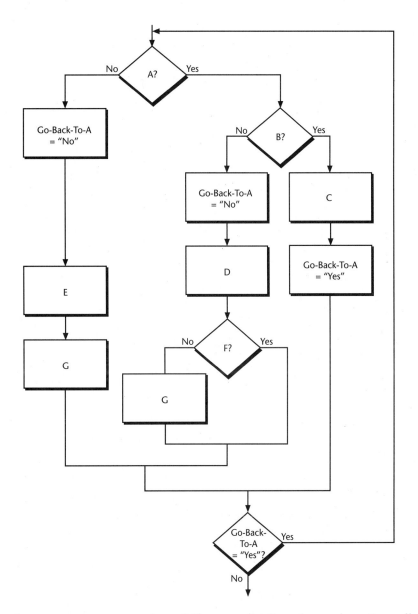

FIGURE A.12

Is this flowchart segment structured now? If you can't tell, make a subroutine called A-THROUGH-G. Is the flowchart segment structured? It's a do-until! (See Figure A.13.)

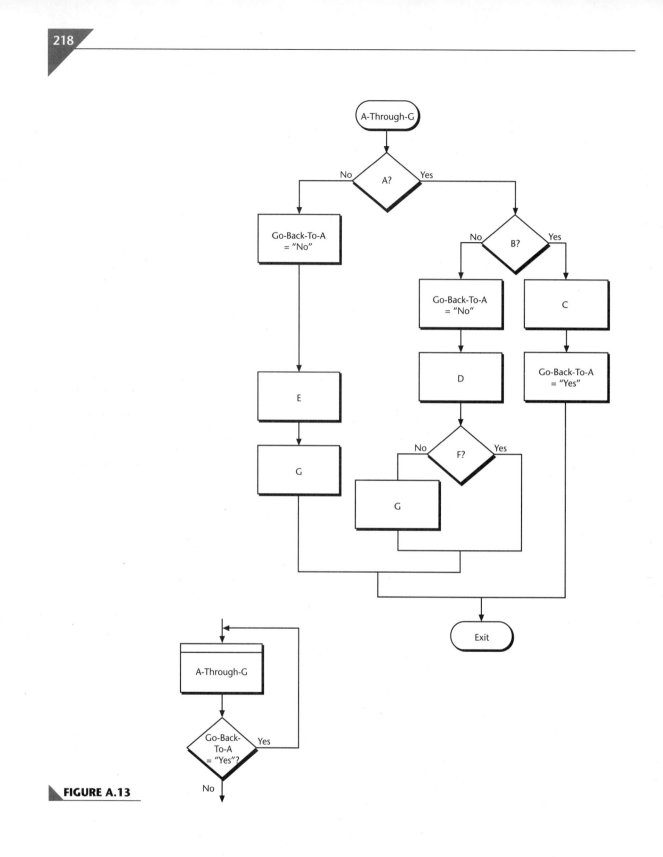

If you don't like do-untils, make it a sequence and a do-while. Either way, the flowchart segment is now structured, with a little help from a flag. (See Figure A.14.)

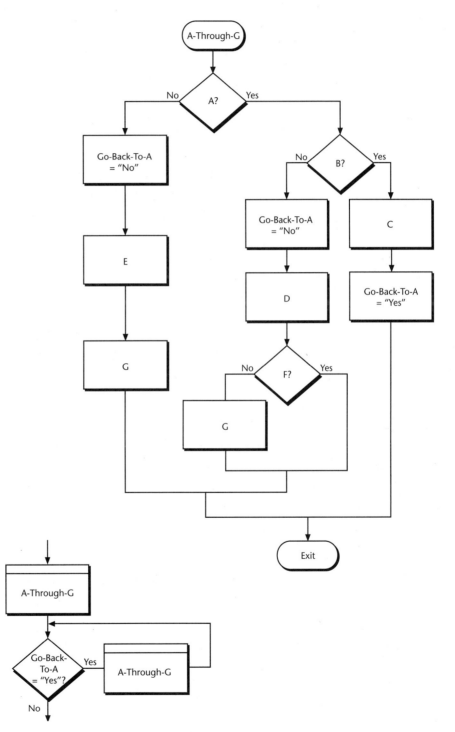

FIGURE A.14

Index